MW01008087

Self-Publishing

Top Ten Tips

JOSEPH JENKINS

Joseph Jenkins Inc.
Grove City, PA

Self-Publishing

Top Ten Tips

ISBN: 978-1-7336035-3-9
Library of Congress Control Number: 2022904757

Published by Joseph Jenkins Inc.
143 Forest Ln., Grove City, PA 16127 USA
Ph: 814-786-9085, Fax: 814-786-8209
Email: Mail@JosephJenkins.com

Distributed by Chelsea Green Publishing, Inc.
85 North Main Street, Suite 120, White River Junction, VT 05001
Ph: 802.295.6300; Fax: 802.295.6444; Orders: 800-639-4099
Office Hours: 9am – 5pm (EST)

Cover design: Joseph C. Jenkins
Cover image modified from AdobeStock #73875042.
Euphorigenic Regular and Freestyle Script fonts used on the cover.
Text paper: 55# Cream 360 ppi
Page layout on QuarkXPress 2022
Proofreading: Eileen M. Clawson
[Any typos were added after proofreading :-)]

Table of Contents

INTRODUCTION

My journey into self-publishing was unusual. I dropped out of grad school in the mid-1990s and decided to turn my graduate thesis into a self-published book. Self-publishing was not my job, and I had never done it. I owned and operated a full-time construction business. I had no formal educational background in English or creative writing. My college degree was in science. The master's program I had nearly finished was in sustainable systems.

At that time, I made a promise to myself: if I ever sell more than a million dollars' worth of my own self-published books, I'll write a small book about how I did it. This is that book. I've hit over three million dollars in book sales, but just haven't had time to devote to this book until now, for reasons that should become clear as you read this.

I also made another promise to myself. Once I started, I would stick with self-publishing for ten years, working, as time allowed, during winters, nights, and weekends. If I wasn't getting anywhere meaningful by then, I'd quit and move on to something else. Here I am, 27 years later and still going strong, and I'm in my 70th orbit around the sun.

I also had no financial backing when I started self-publishing. No advances, no royalties. I was not affiliated with any government agency or academic institution, nor am I today. I had no grants, loans, or inheritances.

I tend to learn things the hard way, sometimes to a fault. Needless to say, I learned a thing or two about self-publishing over these past few decades, and I'm going to summarize in this book what I consider to be the most helpful points.

I wish I could have read a book like this when I was getting started!

The author at an early book signing event (circa 2000).

HERE ARE MY TOP TEN TIPS
(not necessarily in any order)

TIP #1: UNDERSTAND YOUR MOTIVES.

At one time, it was vocational suicide among academic professionals to self-publish anything. If you "had" to self-publish, it may have meant that no one else wanted to publish your work. This would imply that your work was low quality, substandard, useless, maybe even dangerous, revolting, or illegal.

The stigma of self-publishing seemed to confine itself to academic circles and to academically oriented publishers. For example, Huffington Post refers to self-publishers as "the lepers of the literary world," despite the fact that some of the greatest writers of all time self-published at least some of their work, including, for example, Mark Twain, Edgar Allen Poe, e. e. cummings, Beatrix Potter, Benjamin Franklin, William Blake, Walt Whitman, L. Frank Baum, and many others. HuffPost makes it clear that anyone can write and publish anything, no matter how incorrect or misguided (as they clearly demonstrate). Huff adds, "You are not Baum, King, Poe..., Strunk, Twain or just about any one of the famous writers who once dabbled in self-publishing. And...you're not going to be."[1]

Well thanks for the vote of confidence Huff. Maybe readers would rather hear from someone who actually successfully self-publishes, rather than from a declining publication that would eagerly criticize Mark Twain because he had the temerity to *gasp* *self-publish*!

I'm self-publishing *this* book because I have information that I think other people may benefit from. I'm writing for people who are interested in self-publishing but don't know much about it. Your own book idea may be a

[1] https://www.huffpost.com/entry/famous-writers-who-selfpu_b_4303994

memoir, a biography, a children's book, a devotional work, an art book, a textbook, or an instructional manual.

I read several books about self-publishing when I was starting out, but they didn't answer important questions such as how much money do you charge for a book? How much does it cost to print books? How can you succeed as a self-publisher from a business point of view? Where do you get books printed? What about cover art, proofreading, page layout, interior design, photo credits, references, copyrights, ISBNs, LCCNs, bar codes, and so on?

So here we go. Let's talk about the things that HuffPost seems to know little about.

Here are several reasons you would want to self-publish your work:

(a) Because you want to learn how to self-publish. That was my initial reason. I believed that the knowledge I would gain from self-publishing would exceed the value of the master's degree that I would likely never need. Developing a unique skill that could possibly provide a benefit during winter months and off-season schedules seemed like a worthy undertaking. My hunch was correct. I'll explain more about that later.

(b) Because you have unique knowledge that is valuable to only a small number of people. Major publishers aren't interested in putting their time and money behind your passion or your niche topic. My thesis was about "humanure," a word I had to create, a contraction of "human" and "manure." That's what my thesis was about — shit. I believed that no publisher would touch it with a ten-foot shovel, so I didn't even ask. Nevertheless, as I write this, I have directly sold 80,000 copies of the book and continue to sell about 5,000 a year. The book spawned six foreign language print editions (so far) and an additional 12 entire or partial translations in other languages available as eBooks. Plus, the book won numerous awards and is now in its fourth self-published edition. I also wrote three additional books on other subjects in the meantime, both softcover and hardcover, black and white, and color, in my spare time, still employed full-time in the construction trades. This book you're reading now would be my sixth self-published "title."

Allow me to interject here an important fact. Every new book *edition* is considered a brand-new book in the book trade. Each edition has a unique ISBN (International Standard Book Number), and a unique LCCN (Library of Congress Control Number). Minimal changes, or lots of changes, can be made to justify a new edition to a book. Those changes can include new cover art, additional or edited content, different binding, price, subtitles, color versus black and white, and so on. New editions are "front listed" in advertising catalogs, as opposed to backlisted, where older books remain in the back of catalogs and the new books are highlighted in the front. So if you have one book in three editions, you actually have three books. One "title" perhaps, but three distinct books in the book trade.

So technically, I've self-published 12 books when all the editions are taken into consideration. The one you're now reading would be my 13th book.

(c) Because your work would be altered by a publisher in a manner not acceptable to you. Censorship is alive and well in the 21st century. If your subject matter includes political, social, or religious subject matter, health research, medical commentary, personal experiences, or satire that is not popular with the government or the ruling elite, your work can be buried, blocked, canceled, or attacked, if not entirely destroyed, by the major publishers, printers, distributors, and media outlets that are owned or controlled by psychopathic billionaires.

Many successful authors had their books rejected by publisher after publisher because the publishers didn't foresee any real financial return being generated by the books. This is understandable from a business point of view. But your book is your passion, and no one believes in it more than you do. Self-publishing was once difficult. Now it's easy. Once you self-publish your work, you own it, and you control it.

(d) **Because you want a bound printed copy of your work.** Maybe you want your book available in print for posterity. Maybe you just want to write a family memoir and print 20 professional copies for family and friends. Maybe you have a children's book idea and want to try it out and see what kind of reception it gets before diving in deeper.

Digital publications disappear at a flick of a switch. Will anyone a century from now read a digital eBook published today? Not very likely. The life of a print book, on the other hand, can span many generations and can provide a reader with an inside look at what may have been happening way in the past. Lately, I've been reading several books written a century ago about medical issues such as vaccines and infectious diseases. I really appreciate the people who took the time to write these books and the other people who made the effort to keep them in print for so long. They tell stories and reveal information that no medical or big pharma publisher would dare to mention today. Such is the value of a print book.

(e) **Because you like to write.** Some people like to sing. Some like to dance. Some are painters, sculptors, teachers, artists. Writing is an art, and some of us just like doing it. Other people find it difficult and hate doing it; they would rather read than write.

Everyone has his or her own preferences when it comes to reading. I prefer nonfiction. If you like to write mysteries, for example, read mystery books. Some will be good, some won't. Pay close attention to the writing styles and book designs. Copy the good ones, but add your own flair.

Most self-publishers are unlikely to win any Pulitzer Prizes, or get rich and famous, but we will put our thoughts down in writing, and some people will read them and we hope even benefit from them. We might even change someone's life for the better.

Furthermore, self-publishing skills can often develop into photography skills, page layout and design skills, research and continuing education, website development, business skills, computer skills, videography, public speaking, world travel, professional consulting, and development and sales of products related to the subject matter of your writing. My endeavors include all of the above.

There is just something about having a book in your hands, rather than words on a screen. Don't get me wrong, eBooks are fine. You may be reading this as an eBook. You can save your eBook on your device and share it with your friends. You can often cut and paste from it.

But a print book doesn't disappear when the electricity goes out or the battery dies. You don't have to turn on a computer or other electronic device to read it. You can curl up in your favorite chair when all is quiet, glass of wine nearby, and dive into your book. You can give a print book, after you've read it, to friends or family or even leave it for descendants. Or pull it off the shelf weeks, months, or years later, for reference or for inspiration.

One of the worst reasons to start self-publishing is because you want to become rich and famous. Let's take a look at that in the next chapter.

Library of Congress public domain book art from a 1758 book
(https://loc.gov/free-to-use/). An example of how to adapt art like
this to your own book is shown on the next page.

TIP #2:

IF YOU'RE TRYING TO GET RICH, PLAY THE LOTTERY INSTEAD!

If you're self-publishing to get rich, forget it. I'm not trying to discourage you, just giving you a heads-up. There are people who make a lot of money writing and publishing. Usually these are celebrities and public figures who write a quick best seller, make a pile of money, then drop out of the author world. Big publishers will be eager to get your manuscript if you fall into this category.

Then there are the Stephen Kings and the other well-known professional writers who make a fine living writing books and are good at what they do. Stephen King was supposed to have started out self-publishing, but successful self-publishers can often be picked up later by larger publishing firms who see that there is money to be made. My own first two self-published books were requested to be published by larger, established publishers, but I declined the offers. I like self-publishing.

When you self-publish, you don't just write the books; you design them (or you hire a book designer to help you). You create the cover art (or you hire an artist). You do the book indexing, you hire the printer, you inventory or warehouse the books, and you potentially even pack the books up and ship them out. You promote your own books, advertise them, provide an internet presence, communicate directly with your readers, and pay for everything out of your pocket or from your business bank account. When you have a publisher, you simply produce the manuscript, hand it over, and they do the rest.

What's the difference in revenue? A published author may receive a royalty that's somewhere around 7 percent. A self-published author can net around 70 percent through a distributor, and 100 percent of direct sales.

As a self-publisher, I receive, on average, about one-third of the cover price for each book sold. If I've sold three million dollars' worth of books, I've netted one million dollars. If this has taken place over a 25-year span, then I've netted about forty thousand dollars per year, which is nothing to get excited about when you consider that all costs for book production come out of that money. Of course, if it's a part-time, creative side job that you enjoy doing, then the money is a bonus.

My books are distributed by a publisher/distributor called Chelsea Green Publishing. They're great! They receive 30 percent of net sales for any of my books they sell through their distribution. If you're going to sell any quantity of books, you will need a distributor. How did I get a book distributor? They simply called me up one day out of the blue and asked me if they could distribute my first book, my graduate thesis turned "underground best seller." Today there are online companies who will publish and distribute your book for you — companies such as Ingram-Spark, Bowker, and Amazon, to name a few.

A book distributor will market your books to the book trade, to places such as Amazon and Barnes and Noble. These are booksellers who require deep discounts off the cover price, from 40 percent to 60 percent, sometimes more. For example, if you have a $10 book, Amazon may pay your distributor $4.50 for the book. Your book distributor takes 30 percent off that $4.50, leaving you with $3.15/book. This is the money that you receive for your time, your expenses, and your reprints. Looking at these figures, you'd better not be paying more than $1 or $1.50 each to print your $10 books or you'll soon be out of business. This is the reality of publishing.

The Authors Guild surveyed members of 14 writers' organizations in 2018, collecting responses from 5,067 traditional, hybrid, and self-published authors. The respondents reported a median income of only $6,080. This was down 42 percent from 2009, when the median income was $10,500. In 2007, it was even higher at $12,850.

Authors can help bolster their income by supplementing it with work related to their writing, such as speaking engagements, book reviewing, or teaching. By doing this, authors in 2018 had median incomes from all writing related sources of $8,170. This is up from $6,250 in 2013. Full-time book authors still only earned a median income of $20,300, well below the federal poverty level for a family of three or more.

Authors Guild is the nation's oldest and largest professional organization for writers. Its mission is to empower working writers by advocating for the rights of authors and journalists. The Guild protects free speech and authors' copyrights, fights for fair contracts and a living wage, and provides a welcoming community for all authors.

But don't be discouraged about the money. Benefits other than money can be derived from your books. My work developed into two unrelated consulting businesses, one national and one international, allowing me to travel to over 60 foreign countries on business and to supplement my income with consulting fees. The more consulting work I did, the more I learned from it and the more valuable I became as a consultant. Eventually, I acquired enough unique and valuable knowledge that I could create another book. You see where this is going. It doesn't stop.

My publishing work and subsequent internet endeavors birthed a nonprofit international trade association of which I remain executive director. My website work developed into an ecommerce business originally intended to sell books, which mushroomed into internet sales of many items related to the subject matter of the books. I generate a million dollars in sales every year, on average, just from ecommerce alone, with only two people working in the business (I being one of them). The point is that the returns you receive from writing and publishing are not just about money you get from book sales.

You can self-publish with almost no financial risk by using an online publishing platform such as Amazon, Bowker, or IngramSpark. Produce your manuscript in Word, import it into a Kindle converter application on your computer and upload it, and you have a publication on Kindle. Produce the same manuscript in a page layout program such as QuarkXPress or Adobe InDesign, convert it into a PDF (portable document format) using, for example, Adobe Acrobat, then upload it to *Amazon Direct Publishing*. They will print on demand and sell your books for you. You don't have to pay for anything up front other than the business expenses you have in your personal office.

I'm not going to go too deeply into the online publishing platforms or software programs because these things change frequently. They come and go. Best bet is to search online for the latest and greatest options.

IngramSpark provides a calculator allowing you to figure out how much you can earn from the sale of your book. Enter your book's specs (trim size, interior color, paper types, binding, laminate, page count, list price, wholesale discount, and your market area). Select "calculate," and see how much you will make from the sale of one copy of your book.
[https://myaccount.ingramspark.com/Portal/Tools/PubCompCalculator]

TIP #3

GROW A THICK SKIN. YOU'LL NEED IT.

If you're the sensitive type, prepare for your feelings to be hurt. You *will* make mistakes, and they *will* be pointed out. People will not like your work, no matter how good it is, and they *will* be critical and sometimes insulting. This is especially true on the internet.

If your book ends up on Amazon or some other online bookstore, it will likely receive reviews. The more reviews the better — that means people are reading the book and taking the time to review it. However, there are internet trolls who seem to get a perverted pleasure out of giving one-star reviews to books they obviously haven't read. And you can't avoid them. Furthermore, Amazon allows people to post 1-star ratings without identifying themselves or even including a review.

Sometimes you can respond to a troll. One of my books received a 1-star review with the comment that said something like, "The author is so bad he should stick to writing obituaries." I was compelled to write a response: "Thank you for not reading my book. Here is your obituary: *Internet troll found dead in his mother's basement where he lived. He apparently choked to death on cheese puffs and soda pop. The emergency crew had to remove the door jamb to allow for his corpse's excessive mass to squeeze through the door opening.*"

For some reason, Amazon would not post my response. They did, however, eventually delete the 1-star review.

I find it meaningful to look at my work, once published, as if someone else had written it. After all, the guy who wrote it was me in the past. If I had to write it again, it would probably be different because I'm different now.

Some people will like your book, some won't for whatever reason. Welcome people's comments, and learn what you can from them. I've been thankful for almost every comment and whatever feedback I have received, especially legitimate criticism. People will find typos and mistakes, and that's good. You didn't see them, your proofreader(s) didn't catch them, but a reader saw them and was kind enough to point them out for your benefit. Be grateful.

Then there's editing. It's essential that your work be proofread and perhaps edited. What's the difference? A good proofreader will find typos, grammatical irregularities, misspelled names, and other little details that are important. An editor will delete entire paragraphs, rearrange paragraphs or even chapters, substitute words and phrases, make comments about tone and language, and so on. A good editor should be familiar with the subject matter in a non-fiction book, whereas a proofreader doesn't need to be.

I'm not a fan of Microsoft Word. It's not very good for page layout and design. It's clumsy and limited, especially if you are using a lot of photos or images. That being said, Word is great for editing manuscripts. Use the "track changes" feature. The person editing can make the changes directly into the manuscript, but the original wording will remain in place, just crossed over. The writer then gets the edited manuscript back and decides whether each edit makes sense. If it does, she right clicks, "accepts" or "rejects" the change, and it's done. Very convenient.

I enjoy editing with Word and am happy to do it for friends. Sometimes the looks on their faces when they see all of the "mistakes" they made reminds me of the first time my work was edited, and I felt slightly uncomfortable about it. Now I'm totally grateful for anyone to find any mistakes that I may be making.

For example, there are still people who insist on putting two spaces at the end of every sentence when typing.

Yes, we did this in high school typewriter class ages ago, but that doesn't mean it's still done today in print publications. All of those double spaces have to be edited down to a single space. It's annoying.

Another example is where the quotation mark resides in relation to a comma or period. In the UK, the comma or period sits outside the quote mark: "like this". In the US it is inside: "like this." This is why you need a proofreader. I used volunteer friends and family for many years. My dad had an eagle eye. But now I employ a professional proofreader, and she's worth every penny.

Same goes for artists. Admit that they can do a better job of designing a book cover than you can and hire a professional to design your cover if you can afford it. Some people are gifted writers, others are gifted graphic designers. They're worth the money when their work is good and reasonably priced. This does not apply to artists who are publishing their own books and are capable of creating their own artwork. Graphic design services are also available online.

My book cover designer is off on maternity leave, and unavailable as I write this. So I downloaded an Adobe Stock image that cost about $80 and used it to design the cover myself. I altered the image in Photoshop to suit my book size, added my own text and bar code, and ended up with what I hope is an acceptable book cover.

I have other "thick skin" anecdotes on which I could elaborate, such as when Howard Stern's fake dairy farmer verbally attacked me on the Stern radio show, or when Larry the Cable Guy did an episode about my compost toilets followed by an episode about doomsdayers waiting for UFOs to pick them up, as if we were in the same human category (nutjobs?). But, let's move on to Tip #4 instead.

Above is a royalty-free public domain photo of a young lady, taken by Tima Miroshnichenko, and available from Pexels.com. The background was removed, the color image was converted into a "grayscale" image, and a new background was inserted using Photoshop. The background is a public domain library poster from the US Library of Congress. Also, check iStockPhoto and Adobe Stock photos, among others, for images available to self-publishers.

TIP #4

PRACTICE "SHAMELESS SELF-PROMOTION."

This is something many prospective self-publishers do not think about ahead of time. You will have no choice but to become a "shameless self-promoter." This is where "looking at your work as if someone else wrote it" comes in handy. If you don't promote it, who will?

Suppose you're the most beautiful singer in the world. If nobody ever hears your voice, who cares? Art is a form of expression, and expression requires an audience. You're not going to write a book, print copies, then throw them in a box in your garage where nobody will ever read them, are you? What's the point?

That's exactly what I did with my first self-published book. I printed 600 copies. I chose that quantity because that's all I could afford to print. It was a modified master's thesis. No one was going to read it. I wanted to learn how to self-publish, so I ended up with 600 execrable books, and I made almost every mistake you can make producing them. Wrong trim size, terrible images; I wanted to blame the printer for the poor book quality, but it was my own fault. I didn't know what I was doing, and I was learning the hard way. And OK, so I put them in some boxes and stored them in my garage.

Within a week, a friend stopped by, and I gave her a copy, quietly calculating how many years it would take me to give away all my books to those who would take one whether they wanted one or not. Turns out her boyfriend was a reporter for the Associated Press, and he showed up at my front door several days later, with a camera, wanting an interview.

Next thing I knew, there was a gigantic photo of me in

the newspaper poking around in a compost pile with a pitchfork. Presumably, the readers assumed, with horror, that there were human turds in the compost pile. The article went statewide. My niche topic, *humanure*, was both unique and repulsive enough that it unexpectedly piqued the interest of more people than I expected. That crappy first edition, the one I expected to watch rotting in my garage for the rest of my life, garnered a lot of attention and sold 10,000 copies. My self-publishing career was launched.

So, you wrote a book, it's in print, you love it, it's the greatest book in the world. How do you get anyone else interested in it? This is where "shameless self-promotion" comes into play. No, you don't have to walk around beating your chest and bellowing about how fantastic you are as a

Early Associated Press Photo

writer. But you do have to make an effort to at least get the word out that you have a book available and that it may be worth reading to at least some people, if not to everyone on the planet.

Here are the six main ways to do that: email, social media, radio, TV, book signings, and independent publishing organizations (trade organizations are addressed in Tip #8). Being willing to spend time promoting your book or having someone willing to help you with this (think wife, husband, or friend) can make a big difference.

Email

Capture email addresses wherever you can. Add them to your email list. I'm not saying to create spam. You can buy large email lists and become a spammer, but they say spammers evolved directly from primordial slime, and I believe it. Better to invest in an email service such as Mailchimp or Constant Contact. These work well, and you can easily email thousands of people at a time for a reasonable monthly fee. Again, when you're reading this, both of these services may no longer be available, so do a search for any mass email service, and check the user reviews before jumping in too deeply.

There are lots of ways to send promotional emails. Pop out your recording device, and do a quick selfie video of you or something related to your book. Send it out to your email list. Do a video, publish it on an internet video platform, embed it in your website, then send the link to your email list. Received a nice book review recently? Send the quote out to your list. Your emails don't just advertise your product, they remind people that you're still alive, still in business, and still wanting to be in contact with them. If they're not interested, they will unsubscribe.

Social Media

In 2022, video platforms included YouTube, Brand New Tube, Vimeo, Brighteon, Rumble, Bitchute, UgeTube, Odysee, TikTok, and so on. Open accounts in these platforms and use them, although YouTube has recently been banning and deleting videos unfavored by its billionaire controllers. Other social media sites include Telegram, Gab, Parler, Facebook, Instagram, Twitter, Citizen Free Press, Substack, Gettr, and others. Open accounts in these as well, although be aware that Facebook, Instagram, and Twitter have developed a reputation for censorship and propagandizing controversial posts. These social media sites can all be places to get the word out about your book or its content. Who knows what else may be available by the time you're actually reading this book, or, for that matter, how many of the old social media platforms may be gone?

Radio and TV

A lot of what I've done over the years in self-publishing has been by luck or by accident. For example, the first time I attended a publishing trade show, I bumped into an exhibitor who published something like "The Radio and TV Interview Report." What's this, I wondered? Turns out you pay three or four hundred dollars (1998 pricing); they run an ad for your book in their report; it goes to radio and TV studios across the USA, and if anyone is interested in your book, they will call you directly.

My very first call was from the Howard Stern radio show. Of course, he would be interested in human excrement. The way it works is they call you at your house at a scheduled time and you do the radio interview over the phone. So, I sat on my compost toilet, waiting for the early morning "drive time" call, holding it in, so that I could "log out" live on the air in the company of Howard Stern. I wanted to be the very first human being to "download" into a "dry toilet" on the Stern show while politely engaging in conversation, then break the news to Howard and Robin that they were talking to someone who was in the process of laying pipe live on their show. I thought they would be delighted.

It was not to be. After sitting for a half hour waiting, as if I were in some doctor's office, they got on the line and informed me that I had been bumped off the show for a walk-in transvestite. Who can turn down a walk-in trans-vestite at 8 am in New York City? Not the Stern show.

But they did call back a week later to do the interview. I was standing in my bedroom, as the timing was not appropriate for a logout session. The interview was kind of a disaster, so whatever you do, do not listen to the "Feces Farmer" interview on the Howard Stern show, unless you want to hear the little song at the end about midgets engaging in anal intercourse.

One of my few in-studio radio gigs was in Mendocino, California.

I found it interesting that a lot of people did listen to that interview. An old high school friend even emailed me about it, someone I hadn't been in contact with for decades. The interview sold a few books, too.

I did another dozen or so radio interviews just from that one magazine advertisement, all across the US. Many of them were "drive time" interviews, which are the most productive since people are listening while they drive to work. Others were late-night or afternoon interviews. I also did some TV stuff: Home and Garden TV, local public TV and public radio.

My book began as a graduate thesis based on science and research. It was not a joke book, although I did incorporate a number of cartoons (you have to when you're writing about poop). It could be difficult trying to do a serious interview when the interviewer only wants to make fun of the subject matter. However, when it comes to book promotion, all interest is good interest. Bad reviews draw attention to your book. If someone who you think is an idiot (think politician) condemns a book, then it's probably a good book, and you'll want to check it out.

Websites

You should have an internet presence and know how to use it. You should be able to edit your own internet information when you need to, which may be on a daily basis. There are lots of options for hosted websites and blogs.

I prefer to create and maintain my own websites rather than have them hosted by website providers, sort of a website self-publishing perspective. This can sometimes be problematic because the internet and associated protocols are changing constantly. Your website will need to change accordingly, so if your website platform is managed by a third party, they will take care of keeping the platform up-dated, but they're not going to update your personal information. You still have to do that.

Alternatively, you can purchase the services of a managed Virtual Private Server (a VPS, or shared server) or a managed Private Server, which is a computer, hosted by a third party, that you use exclusively. Private servers are more secure, but also more expensive.

If you're using a website service, all of the software and resources are included. If you're making your own websites, you will need a website editing program, such as Adobe Dreamweaver, and a file transfer program such as WS_FTP. You keep your website on your own office computer, change it as you need it, and upload the changes to your server whenever you want to.

A server is a big computer owned and managed by someone else. I'm currently using three different website hosting services: Liquid Web, Dathorn, and X-Cart. There are hundreds available. I have used many, but these three have been stable and reliable for years; otherwise I wouldn't mention them. And no, I do not receive anything for mentioning products or companies in this book.

Servers are computers that house your website and almost everyone else's. Bigger companies have their own servers and manage them in house. You access your server using username and password credentials via an FTP software (File Transfer Protocol) over Wi-Fi. That's how you keep your website updated.

Your website's address is defined by a Uniform Resource Locator (URL), which points to the server where your website resides.

Your actual domain name (yourname.com) is registered with a domain name registrar. I use Moniker.com, but there are hundreds of options, some good, some bad. At the domain name registrar, you plug in your server host names, also known as name servers. For example: host1@nameserver.com and host2@nameserver.com, where your website is hosted. When someone types in your domain name online, the registrar makes sure it goes to your host server.

This seemingly convoluted process enables you to register a domain name at a registrar, point it to a host server, and create your own independently controlled web presence without having to go through a website development service.

One advantage to using your own host server and creating your own websites is that when you buy a host server package, you're buying disk space and bandwidth. Disk space is how many gigabytes of room you have to work with on the server computer. Bandwidth is how much traffic can run through your website at one time. You need a lot more bandwidth if you're streaming video content, for example.

You're not buying a website but renting a place to have your website(s) hosted. You can have as many websites as you want on your host server at no additional charge as long as you're not exceeding your disk space or bandwidth limit. If you have simple one-page "landing pages" or other small websites, you can have a lot of them, all with different domain names. You can have mybookrocks.com, mybookisgreat.com, stuffrelatedtomybook.com, theauthor.com, mybusiness.com, and so on. All are stand-alone websites, and all would be linked together by internal links.

Here's a trick that many people don't know. Search engines rank your website higher if it's linked to other sites. If you don't have links to your site or from your site, then it's a stagnant site. If you have several sites of your own, you can crosslink them and boost your search engine ratings. Let's say you have a book about baby dolls. You would have a website mybabydollbook.com. Then you'd have another website about baby dolls (babydolls.com) and cross link it to your book site. Then maybe you'd start selling baby dolls or baby doll parts, so you'd have another website called babydollstore.com. You get the idea.

Here's another trick. OK, so you bought the domain name babydoll.com. Buy the same domain name with additional extensions (.net, for example). Buy babydolls.com, too. Maybe buy baby-doll.com and dollbaby.com.

I had bought the domain name slateroofers.org for a nonprofit organization. I was on the phone with an architect talking about the organization, and I suggested he check out the website. As he was saying goodbye, he said he would check it out – slatecontractors.org. No, I corrected him, *slateroofers.org,* hung up, and immediately bought the slatecontractors.org domain name. Also slateroofers.com, slatecontractors.com, slatecontractor.org, and so on. Buy up all the permutations of your domain name. Register them with your registrar (which is where you buy them). Point them to your host server, then "park" them there as "alias" domains. If people type in the wrong domain name, they will still end up at your site!

One other thing about websites for those of you who have little experience in this subject. Note that the URL has either an http:// prefix or an https:// prefix. The one with the "s" signifies a "secure" website, one where you can make use of passwords, credit cards, and so on. In order to have a secure site, you have to install what's called an SSL certificate (Secure Sockets Layer). This is done through your website control panel (cPanel), which you have access to when you create your own websites. You can buy SSL "certs" online. Some are more expensive than others. Digicert is a good company, although relatively expensive.

I don't want to get too far into the weeds with websites and the internet because this could involve another entire book, one that would need to be updated annually. The point is that you should do your homework and figure out how to achieve an effective and lasting web presence. Then maintain it and keep it updated. You can limit yourself to social media sites, or pay for a website service, or get a host server and create your own website(s), or all of the above.

Public Speaking

You're scared already; I can tell. The National Social Anxiety Center says that "the fear of public speaking is the most common phobia, ahead of death, spiders, and heights. The National Institute of Mental Health reports that public speaking anxiety, or glossophobia, affects about 73 percent of the population."

People *would rather die* than speak in public. It's an irrational fear. I know, I had it, but not anymore. Once you figure out how to get over it, public speaking is fun. It's a valuable, empowering skill, like self-publishing. Maybe I'll write another book about public speaking tips. You know: "Public Speaking: Top Ten Tips for the Terror-Stricken."

Public speaking provides lots of benefits other than just promoting your book or whatever by-products you have that are related to your book's content. For example, if you write a book about baby dolls, you can realistically posture yourself as an expert on baby dolls. You did the work and the research that sets you apart from everyone else. Your baby doll acumen enables you to know which baby dolls are the best and which are the worst. You can use your skills to select top quality baby dolls and offer them for sale. "Choice" baby dolls, so to speak. Bring your books with you to a speaking engagement and bring some of the baby dolls, too. Use some for display during your presentation, and keep the rest on a table in the back of the room where they can be available for purchase.

Speaking engagements will give you the opportunity to make new friends, meet people, travel, get recognized both as an expert and as a public speaker, and garner new and unexpected opportunities. Let me give you an example.

I got a phone call from the United States Department of Agriculture (USDA) a while back. The man, let's call him Jim, was inviting me to speak at a USDA conference about "Composting Dairy Manure." He was organizing the conference, and his girlfriend had read my thesis book about humanure. She handed him the book and told him, "Jim, try to get this guy as a speaker for the conference."

I said to Jim on the phone, "I don't compost dairy manure. I compost human manure. I have relatives large enough to pass as dairy animals, but that's as close as I get to dairy manure. My cousin Larry's a horse's ass. He poops. Does that count?" I told him to let me think about it.

One of the rules of public speaking is "Know Your Material." Unless you're a politician, don't get up in front of a group of people and try to give a speech about something you know nothing about. That's when you get halfway through a sentence, forget what you're talking about, and everybody is staring at you like they're seeing a person

A public speaking engagement titled, "Close Encounters of the Turd Kind." Note the rapt attention.

about to be run over by a car. That's a recipe for disaster, unless you're a comedian and can ad-lib effectively.

Jim said there would be about 150 people attending the conference, including the mayor of the town hosting the event. It would last all day, with a lunch provided. The five speakers would each be required to give a separate speech. The rest of the day the five of us would sit on a panel, on an elevated stage, taking questions from the audience.

I wrestled with the idea for a few days. I had never composted dairy manure. I would be stupid to get in front of an audience and pretend to know what I was talking about. It would be a mistake to accept the invitation. On the other hand, I needed to practice public speaking. I had been to numerous farms where dairy manure was being composted. I did take a week long "Master Composter" course in Nova Scotia, Canada, that included some time on a dairy farm. Maybe I could practice telling jokes. Based on that imbecilic shred of rationality, I agreed to speak.

When it was my turn to address the audience, I informed them I had never composted dairy manure, told them about my rotund relatives and my cousin Larry, then admitted that when manure is composted, even human manure, it becomes a benign, odorless material safe to freely handle with bare hands. You can even roll around in it naked without reservation. I announced that we had laid out a tarp in the dining room here at the conference, dumped compost on it, and that Jim, the USDA conference organizer who was standing in the back of the room, was going to roll around in the compost without any clothes on while we were eating our lunch, just to prove the point.

Jim never did invite me to speak anywhere else ever again. But during lunch a lady sat next to me, and we struck up a conversation. She was the Pennsylvania state organizer for compost and agriculture. Would I agree to be a speaker at the upcoming Pennsylvania composting conference in the state capital, she asked? Why, sure, why not. I agreed. This time, I elected to speak about the Canadian province of Nova Scotia's cutting-edge composting operations. I flew back up to Canada, interviewed everyone involved, recorded it all in a document, produced a PowerPoint presentation, and delivered it in Harrisburg, the capital of Pennsylvania. It was well received.

I then took that documentation, submitted it to the US Composting Council as a potential topic for their national conference, and they accepted it. My next speaking engagement was at a national venue, all because I agreed to take a speaking engagement about dairy manure. I went on to speak several times at national venues, then international venues multiple times. I wasn't necessarily plugging my book, but I was meeting a lot of new people, gaining name recognition, learning a lot, and having a good time traveling. I subsequently wrote additional nonfiction books and developed somewhat of a background in public speaking. I was comfortable accepting speaking engagements nationwide. Even overseas.

The point I'm trying to make here is that sometimes you have to take a chance and hope for the best. Practice, practice, practice. If you fall, get up. Do it again. Get up again. Don't expect everything to happen all at once either. Allow yourself some time to develop your skills. Years perhaps. Perseverance pays.

Public speaking is like riding a bicycle. The first time you try it you'll be a bit wobbly and may even fall over. It may be embarrassing. You may laugh at yourself. Others may laugh at you. You get back up and try again. You may fall over several times. Maybe even get scraped up and draw blood. Put a Band-Aid on, get back on the bicycle, and try again. Start small and work your way up. Eventually it will become second nature. Public speaking will be easy, and you'll learn to enjoy it, just like riding a bicycle. Trust me.

Videos

It's pretty easy these days to video record just about anything at any time. Videos are great marketing tools. I have already listed numerous online video platforms that are freely available. Record video, edit it, upload it, and advertise it by sending links to the video via email, or by embedding videos on your website. You can both promote your product and provide useful information for the general public by using video footage.

Free Downloads

Here's a promotional tip that you're not going to see anywhere else. It involves copyrights. I'm not recommending that you do this; I'm just divulging some of my personal experiences.

A standard copyright would be something like this: "Copyright © 2022 by Joseph C. Jenkins. All rights reserved. Neither this book nor any parts within it may be sold or reproduced in any form without permission."

Since my first book wasn't about my making money, this is how I worded the copyright notice (here paraphrased): "Copyright Joseph C. Jenkins. All rights reserved. The author permits the use of substantial excerpts from this book, providing that the use of such excerpts is not for the purpose of financial profit, the information is not altered or changed, and the source of the information is acknowledged. This license is granted to make information in this book available to those people who cannot afford to purchase an entire book."

My book was written not to make money, but to provide information. I didn't care if I made a penny on the book, although it would be nice to at least break even on expenses. This reminds me of an old adage that states, "Don't worry about money. Do good work, and the money will follow." The adage isn't that old since I made it up, but it seems to be true. Focus on the quality and meaning of your work. Don't worry about how much money you're making. I guarantee that the better your work gets, the more people will be wanting to throw money at you to do work for them. *Guaranteed*.

Before long, I got a phone call from a young man asking me if he could put my entire book on the internet so people could download it for free. I was at first a bit startled by the question as it was something I had never considered. Who would buy my print book if anyone could just download the material for free, I wondered? After all, I was hoping to break even on expenses. "Let me give that some thought," I told the website geek. "I'll get back to you."

I discussed the issue with friends and family, seeking advice, but nobody knew what to say. I thought it over for a few days, then decided, what the hell. Why not? I called the young man back, gave him the go-ahead, and the newly published second edition of the book was up online for anyone to read from that point on. That was the year 2000. It was still online 22 years later at WebLife.org.

To make a long story short, it *increased* book sales. Readers saw the book online, liked what they saw, then bought hard copies. I wouldn't have believed it if I hadn't experienced it myself.

Book Signings

Sometimes book signings can be great. Other times they can be a total waste of time. One of my friends had a small store in a local town, and she asked me if I would do a book signing there. Of course, I agreed. We sent out press releases to the local newspapers. This was my first book signing, and I had no idea what to expect. It took place on a Sunday. The store opened at 9 a.m. I made a quick stop at a convenience store on the way to the book signing and picked up a copy of the *New York Times* and a cup of coffee, assuming I would have a lot of time waiting around and I'd have something to read in the meantime.

To make another long story short, I never even cracked the paper open. People started arriving at 9 a.m. and came in, one after the other, all day long. I wasn't overrun with people, but I was constantly busy. We sold books. A percentage went to the store, and everyone was happy.

After that, I thought it would be a good idea to organize my own book signings. I got a bookstore in downtown Philadelphia to host me. I designed a flier and mailed it to all of the architectural firms in Philadelphia (the book was about an architectural topic). I took a couple of cases of books with me, set up a table in the bookstore, laid out some books and some literature, and waited. And waited. I should have brought a copy of the *New York Times* with me. Nobody showed up. I may have sold one or two books. It was a bust.

I've done a few other book signings since then, by invitation, and they've been mostly mediocre. Some were a complete waste. However, book signings do provide an opportunity to meet people, especially at conferences. So, if you get a chance, at least give it a try.

TIP #5

KNOW YOUR MATERIAL!

If you don't know your subject matter, you shouldn't be writing about it, or publishing books or articles about it. The best self-published books are written by people with personal first-hand knowledge of the subject matter. I'm a non-fiction writer, so don't expect me to give you much advice about fiction work such as novels or children's books. I would advise that you consider taking courses or workshops in creative writing, English grammar, that sort of thing. If you don't want to do that, or can't for some reason, conduct independent research and education by reading books, watching videos and documentaries, listening to podcasts and interviews, reviewing research papers if applicable, or maybe do online or classroom courses.

If you're writing about your experiences, you don't have to read any books beforehand. But you should have a dictionary and a thesaurus at your fingertips. If you're writing on a computer, it's easy to check an online dictionary or thesaurus for word corrections or options.

The fourth edition of my thesis book required that I read or review a stack of printed reference material about 5 feet high, plus scores of papers and manuscripts on my computer. Which reminds me, 5 feet is about 1.5 meters. When writing, understand that your readers may live in other countries where the metric system is standard. When you tell Americans that something is 72 centimeters long, they respond with a blank stare. When you tell a German that something is 15 ½ inches long, same thing. If you think your work is going to be read outside the US, consider including metric conversion in parentheses after the "Imperial" numbers.

Example used in a sentence: "The average human brain weighs about 4 pounds (1.8 kg), unless you're my cousin Larry, who is lucky if he has 2 pounds (0.9 kg) of functional brain tissue."

I once threw an entire book into my woodburning stove after reading only the first chapter. The information was simply incorrect. I knew more about the subject matter than the author did. The egregious errors in those initial pages indicated that the remainder of the book was not worth reading. Don't let that be your book.

If you're not going to employ a proofreader or editor, then lasso up some friends and relatives who will volunteer their time to look through your work. If they have a background in English, editing, or writing, then you're lucky. Even if they don't, they can still provide useful feedback on content, tone, language, illustrations, interior and cover design, and other elements of your book.

When I had drafted my first self-published book manuscript, I thought I'd give it to an artist friend to see if he could come up with some ideas for illustrations. I dropped off the typewritten manuscript at his house, gave him some ideas of what I had in mind for illustrations, told him to take his time and look through the manuscript to get the gist of the content, and let me know what he thought.

About a week later he walked into my house, manuscript in hand, lifted it over his head and slammed it on the kitchen table. "I wouldn't touch this with a 10-foot pole!" he stammered. "You're going to get sued if you publish this. You'll lose your property and maybe everything you own! No, thanks. Count me out!" Then he turned around and walked out just as quickly as he had walked in. I am not making this up.

I admit, that shook me up a bit and threw a little cold water on my fledgling self-publishing career. I soon regained my composure and decided to take my chances and forge ahead with the predicted lawsuits. The lawsuits never happened, but thanks to that AP reporter, lots of interest developed, and the book sold. My artist friend calmed down when he saw that the book was being well received, and his illustrations graced all future editions.

To provide another example of how friends can be involved with your work, I gave a draft manuscript to one of my neighbors. She had a master's degree and was willing to proofread the document. The only thing in the entire book that needed attention, in her opinion, was a comment I made that she thought was disrespectful. I said something about public health inspectors being clueless about compost. Maybe I said they didn't know something from Shinola, or maybe something about their rear end and a hole in the ground; I don't remember the exact wording. But you know, she was right. There's no point in unnecessarily offending people. So I changed it to say that public health inspectors are not trained in compost science or management, hence they know little about the subject. Definitely an improvement to my book. Thank you, neighbor.

There are some writing standards and styles in literature that you may want to know about, such as the APA style, the Chicago style, the MLA style, and others.

For many college students, the standard writing and citation style guidelines are found in the *Publication Manual of the American Psychological Association*, also known as APA style. This style provides "generally accepted rules for writing, publication conventions, and best practices for research, methodology, and ethics of authorship for writers, educators, and editors in the behavioral and social sciences." We had to use this style in graduate school.

If you're citing reference sources from research you've conducted, then you should follow one style or another.

The APA style tends to be used with education, psychology, and sciences subject matter. The MLA style (Modern Language Association) tends to be used in the humanities genre (history, philosophy, religion, languages, literatures, arts, media, cultural studies, and other fields). The Chicago/Turabian style is generally used by business, history, and the arts.

Here is a book citation in APA style:
Author Last name, First initial. Middle initial. (Year Published). *Title of work.* Publisher.

Sapolsky, R. M. (2017). *Behave: The biology of humans at our best and worst.* Penguin Books.

Here's a Chicago style book reference:
Author first name last name, *Book Title: Subtitle* (Place of publication: Publisher, Year), Page number(s).

Michael Pollan, *The Omnivore's Dilemma: A Natural History of Four Meals* (New York: Penguin, 2006), 99–100.

Here is an MLA style book reference:
Author's last name, First name. *Title of the Book.* Publisher, Year published.

Card, Claudia. *The Atrocity Paradigm: A Theory of Evil.* Oxford University Press, 2005.

A good proofreader is going to stick to one style or another, and he or she will make sure all of your reference citations, assuming you have any, will be done exactly as the style requires.

TIP #6:

START SMALL, DAMMIT!

As wonderful as your book is, it may bomb. This is the harsh reality of any kind of publishing. Professional publishers will have a good idea of what will sell and what won't. They know the market, the trends, the fads and inclinations of the consumers, or at least they hope they do. It's one thing to underestimate a book and have to print more. That's not a problem. You may be out of stock for a brief time, although if you keep an eye on inventory and watch your sales, you can stay ahead of the curve.

It's when you overestimate your book's appeal and print too many copies that you end up in an embarrassing situation. One reason this becomes a complication among self-publishers is that the more books you print, the less they cost per book. Five thousand copies of a 300-page black-and-white book may cost you only $2 each to have printed and bound. Yet a 25-page black-and-white booklet will cost you $5 each when you only print fifty.

When you get quotes from printers for your book project, you'll find that if you add that extra thousand copies or more, the price per unit drops significantly. It's very tempting to convince yourself that the book is going to be well received, popular, and a sales success, so why not? Let's double the print run!

You probably didn't see the documentary about the new self-publisher who wrote a nonfiction book about his personal life, with a focus on relationships. The book was poignant, meaningful, touching, and full of wisdom and advice that everyone would benefit from. So he printed 7,000 copies, went on a speaking tour wherever he could schedule anything, advertised as much as he could, knocked on doors, promoted his book till he was blue in the face, and sold about a thousand copies. We'll get back to him in a minute.

According to Tucker Max on ScribeMedia.com, the average self-published, *digital-only* book only sells about 250 copies in its lifetime. The average traditionally published book sells 3,000 copies in its lifetime, but only about 250 to 300 of those sales happen in the first year. For a traditional publisher to think of a nonfiction book as a success, it must sell more like 10,000 copies over its lifetime.

To hit a home run publishing your book, your first week's sales have to reach 500 copies (industry average is 50). Your first-quarter sales would have to reach 1,000 copies (industry average is 200). Your daily average sales would have to be 6 to 10 copies (industry average is 0 to 2). Your first-year sales would have to reach at least 2,500 books (industry average is 400). A home run in book sales over a five-year period would have to be at least 5,000 copies sold. The industry average is 1,000.

Bowker's *Self-Publishing in the United States, 2013—2018*, revealed that the combined total of registered self-published print books and eBooks grew from almost 1.2 million in 2017 to more than 1.6 million in 2018, a 40 percent increase. Compare this to 2013, when the number of registered print books and eBooks was only 461,438.

"The self-publishing landscape continues to improve, creating more and more opportunities for authors to manage their own path through the process," according to Beat Barblan, VP of Publishing and Data Services at Bowker and chairman of the board of the International ISBN Agency. "As more authors take advantage of the abundant tools now available to publish, distribute, and market their own books, we expect that self-publishing will continue to grow at a steady pace."

That means there is a lot of competition in the self-publishing world. Many self-published works now rival traditionally published titles in quality and appeal. Authors have access to a wide range of professional services, from editing and proofreading to cover and interior design. By taking advantage of these opportunities, along with online marketing and distribution services, self-published authors are more likely to succeed than ever before.

The fellow who printed 7,000 copies did pretty well selling about a thousand copies of his book that first year. But then he had 6,000 copies to get rid of. They were stacked in so many boxes in his garage he didn't have room to park his car. He ended up standing on sidewalks on college campuses with his girlfriend handing out books for free to any passerby who would take one. You don't want to put yourself in that situation.

Could you donate excess book to libraries? Prisons? Maybe. My thesis book's first edition, first printing, was a horrible book. Like I said, I made every mistake you can make as a self-publisher. Yet it sold 10,000 copies in three printings over a couple of years. People in the know told me this was pretty good for a first self-published book, so I decided to do a second edition.

In the next edition I cleaned up the book and added a nice new cover and a color photo section. I even had a color photo of a man bent over "shooting the moon" in my garden (it wasn't me — I took the photo…trust me…). The "moon" was obvious if you knew where to look, but cleverly hidden at the same time. As far as I know, nobody ever noticed it or any of the other hidden gems I had slipped into the second edition. My artist friend's cartoon artwork graced this edition, too.

The book won numerous book awards and was deemed "most likely to save the planet" in one award ceremony.

That's also when people started asking me if they could translate the book and publish it in foreign countries. I initially gave away the translation rights for free. The first foreign edition was in South Korea. The second was in Israel.

If you think I'm telling you all this to brag, I am not. My mother proudly took a copy of the second edition of my now award-winning, translated, self-published book to her local library in her hometown of Sierra Vista, Arizona. She donated it to the library, proud to be able to hand over a book written by her own son. They promptly handed it right back to her, rejecting the donation. "This book does not meet our community standards," they curtly informed her. I wouldn't have cared if they had rejected the book under any other circumstances, but directly from the hand of my own mother?

So, can you donate books to libraries? Maybe, maybe

Actual quote from a city librarian in Arizona.

This illustration is from the *Humanure Handbook*, fourth edition.

not. Depends on what kind of mood they're in, I guess. In fairness, many libraries did stock a copy of that book. My local university library has a copy that's been checked out so many times, it's falling apart.

One way to start small is with an eBook. Kindle, for example. Then try a print-on-demand edition through, for example, Kindle Direct Publishing. There may be dozens of similar options available. Otherwise, start with a small printing. If you think the book will do well, print 500 or a thousand. If it does well, print 5,000 at a time. Your price per book will come way down as print quantities go up.

Let me sneak in here another trick for self-publishers that no one seems to know about. You're writing nonfiction, let's say about baby dolls, and there's a pretty big baby doll industry in your country. You have already published the book's first edition, and it has proven its popularity. Now you're ready to do a new edition. Leave a number of pages blank at the end of the book just in front of the index. Offer these pages to advertisers in the industry. Give them the option of a quarter page, half page, whole page, or two-page spread. This is the sort of thing you can do as a self-publisher that a dedicated publisher or an academic publisher would never dream of doing.

One of my books was a full-sized 8.5" × 11" softbound trade book in full color with 590 illustrations and 316 pages. This was an expensive book to print. By attending trade shows, I discovered that I could print it in Hong Kong for much less than US printers would charge. I added ten blank pages in the back of the book, sold the advertising to interested parties in the industry, and actually made a profit on the book printing of $17,000. You heard that right. I had $17,000 left over *after* the book was printed.

I took that money and bought a "made in the USA" piece of heavy equipment, which helped appease everybody who was shocked that I would print overseas (all my other books have been printed in the USA).

The next edition of the same book was a hardcover version in full color with nearly 800 illustrations in 374 pages that cost me $40,000 to print. Again, I had it done in Hong Kong (TSE Worldwide Press Inc.). I sold 10 pages of full-color ads in the back of the book at an average of $8,000 per page, grossing over $80,000 in ad revenue, and clearing $40,000 in profit before the first book even hit the bookshelves. All of the ads were indexed, too.

That's another thing, the index. You don't need an index for a novel or a children's book, but most nonfiction books should be indexed as it greatly improves the quality of a nonfiction book. Some publishing software such as QuarkXPress includes a book feature with an indexing component. After you've completed the book, you mark the words you want indexed, and Quark compiles them for you into an index file with the correct page numbers.

The book you're reading now was created in Quark so you can see what I'm talking about. I produced the initial manuscript in Word, cut and pasted it into Quark, finalized the editing, then applied the final formatting. Quark is great but expensive. I got a discounted version as a college student and have been updating and using it ever since. It's a bit of a learning curve, but it's powerful and versatile.

Adobe InDesign (once known as Adobe PageMaker) is a popular competitor to Quark. It's less expensive and can come bundled with the very useful Adobe Creative Cloud Suite. I can't comment on InDesign because I've never used it, even though I have it in my Creative Cloud Suite. Once you start publishing using a certain page-layout software and a certain computer platform (Mac or PC), it's easier to stick with what you're used to than to switch to an entirely new program or platform.

TIP #7:

Use The Correct Software.

We partially covered this issue with our discussion about Quark and InDesign as page layout applications. But there are a number of other software types that are essential to making your work easier. One is a good PDF application that will convert your manuscript into a PDF version, thereby enabling you to upload it to your website, where it can be downloaded, either for free or for a fee. I use Adobe Acrobat, but there are others.

Acrobat allows you to edit PDF documents and save them as high-quality print files that can be uploaded or FTP'd to your printer's website.

You should also have a file sharing application available, such as Dropbox, so you can upload your chapters, your entire book, your book's illustrations, and so on, and then share the files with anyone of your choosing (such as your proofreader, editor, or illustrator).

If you're doing any number of illustrations, you will need software for that purpose. I'm partial to Photoshop, but there are many others, depending on your computer platform and your personal preferences. Color illustrations in books print using a four-color process, also known as CMYK (cyan, magenta, yellow, black). Color illustrations for eBooks are three-color, or RGB (red, green, blue). When you save photos or illustrations for book printing, they must be in a CMYK mode. Converting images to CYMK is easy in Photoshop. Simply change the image mode.

When I started self-publishing in the mid-1990s, I started writing on pen and paper. Hey, if it worked for Ben Franklin, it should work for me. But then it all had to be rewritten to get it into a format that a printer could use.

So I upgraded to an electronic typewriter. That way I could type in my text and save it on the meager memory that was internal to the typewriter. I could do nothing with illustrations, however, on a typewriter.

Personal computers were not common at that time, but they were becoming increasingly available. I assembled my first computer on the floor of my small office with the help of a geek friend. We bought the motherboard and other components separately, put them together, and managed to get a working computer up and running to replace the electronic typewriter. Now I could do the text and the illustrations together through a page layout application.

The problem was backing up the files. The price of memory at that time was $60/Mb. A 10-megabyte memory card cost $600. Now you can buy a 64-gigabyte memory card for $20. Back then, we had back-up tape drives that backed up data on what looked like cassette tapes. You would set the computer to back up your data, then walk away for an hour while the tape backed up your files. That's how slow it was. It was either that or lose all your data if the computer failed or even if the power went out in the middle of a file backup.

The internet was deplorable back then, too. Many a time when I needed to download a sizeable internet file I would start the download at bedtime, get up in the middle of the night to see if it was still downloading, then go back to bed and hope it had completed by morning. Often, the internet connection had broken in the night, and I would have to start the download over again the next day, from the beginning. There was an electric fence along the road a half mile away that sometimes crackled in the night, maybe from deer or a cow brushing against it. That crackle was enough to break the internet connection running through the overhead phone line.

We've come a long way since then, and now writing and publishing is easier than ever. Don't do things the hard way because sooner or later you're going to get wise and upgrade everything to make it easier for yourself. Invest in a decent computer, and use the correct software. Take the time to learn how to use them. You will be making first-class publications in no time.

Another bit of advice: Don't try to do everything yourself. Get help when you need it and not just with editing and proofreading. There are great artists who will change your book from OK to wonderful. They have their own software, and they know how to use it.

Speaking of artists, make sure you have a signed contract with them so that you own their artwork when you pay for it. The term is called "work for hire." The terms of the contract should include that you not only own the artwork, but that you can use the artwork in any format, in any publication, at any time, and you can alter the artwork to suit your needs. Here's an example of wording for a cover art agreement. Consult your attorney for updates:

This is an Agreement between [NAME], hereinafter Artist, normally doing business at [ADDRESS], as a Freelance Graphic Designer, and [BUYER OF ART], normally doing business at [ADDRESS]. This Agreement covers the preparation of cover art for the book [NAME OF BOOK], further described in attached image, and submission of ideas and materials therefor. Artist will deliver to [BUYER] on or before [DATE], the cover art for the book [NAME OF BOOK], in form and content satisfactory to [BUYER]. Artist is an independent contractor. This work is considered work-for-hire under the United States Copyright Act of 1976. All concepts, ideas, copy, sketches, artwork, electronic files, and other materials related to it will become the property of [BUYER]. Artist acknowledges that cover art for the book [BOOK] is being created by Artist for use by [BUYER]. At [BUYER]'s sole and absolute discretion, [BUYER] may make any changes in, deletions from, or additions to cover art for the book [BOOK]. [BUYER] is not under any obligation to use cover art for the book [BOOK] or derivative materials. Artist acknowledges that cover art for [BOOK] is being created by artist for use by [BUYER] and that cover art for the book [BOOK] is a work made for hire under the United States Copyright Act of 1976. At all stages of development, the cover art for the book [BOOK] shall be and remain the sole and exclusive property of [BUYER]. If for any reason the results and proceeds of Artist's services hereunder are determined at any time not to be a work made for hire, Artist hereby assigns to [BUYER] all right, title, and interest therein, including all copyrights as well as renewals and extensions thereto. Credit for the work shall read: "Cover design based on artwork by [ARTIST'S NAME]," provided that a substantial portion of Artist's work is used in [BUYER'S] final product. No inadvertent failure by [BUYER] to comply with the credit line shall constitute a breach of this Agreement. Artist represents and warrants to [BUYER] that to the best of her knowledge the concepts, ideas, copy sketches, artwork, electronic files, and other materials produced do not infringe on any copyright or personal or proprietorial rights of others, and that she has the unencumbered right to enter into this Agreement. Artist will indemnify [BUYER] from any damage or loss, including attorney's fees, rising out of any breach of this warranty. Artist grants [BUYER] the right to issue and authorize publicity concerning Artist and to use Artist's name and approved biographical data in connection with the distribution and advertising of the project. Any proprietary information, trade secrets and working relationships between Artist and [BUYER] and its clients must be considered strictly confidential, and may not be disclosed to any third party, either directly or indirectly. Please indicate acceptance of the terms above by signing this Agreement.

If you want to use a contributed photo, drawing, or image that you are *not* paying for, then it's not work for hire. You still must have the rights to use the image, in writing. If your book is about baby dolls and someone offers you an adorable photo they took of their baby doll, you can use it, but you need written permission. You are not free to use anyone's photo or image without a license, except in rare cases. You can't even paint or draw a modified rendition of someone else's photo and then claim your own work for commercial purposes without fear of legal retribution from the person who took the photo.

Here's an example of how to word such a license, although you can probably get a better version from a lawyer. You should have a separate license for each image, to be safe. In any case, the images must be visibly included on the signed agreement form. You *can* do this for multiple images and put photos all on one form if needed. Note that the ownership of the original image remains with the original artist/photographer, and they can make the image available to others if they so choose:

> [Artist's Name] hereby attests that I/we are the owner of the copyright to the image(s) below [show image(s) underneath the text]. I/we hereby grant to [Author's name], a nonexclusive, worldwide, perpetual, royalty-free license to distribute, modify, create derivative works based on, publicly perform, publicly display, and otherwise use or publish the photo(s) or image(s) in any format, and to reproduce, distribute and display for commercial or personal use, in any size, style, or publication, either electronic, in print form, on any media, or on the internet, the images shown below. Ownership rights will remain with the owner. No payment or other compensation for the use of the image(s) is due other than to receive a free copy of [Your Book], upon publication, and to credit the source of the image in any book or magazine in which the image is used in its entirety. Credit for the images should read as follows: [].

Here is a list of the software programs I use on a regular, if not daily, basis. This is for PCs. Many of these programs may be available for Macs:

QuarkXPress: page layout, word processing

Adobe Photoshop: image editing

Adobe Acrobat: conversion to PDF

Adobe Dreamweaver: website creation and editing

WS_FTP Pro: file transfer to server

Microsoft Word: word processing, editing

Firefox: web browsing (there are many others)

Notepad: Great for cutting and pasting from Word or from the internet to delete unseen formatting.

Adobe Premiere Pro: video editing

Wondershare AllMyTube: video downloading

Microsoft Office: PowerPoint, Excel, etc.

Adobe Creative Cloud: all the Adobe products are included here

Dropbox: file sharing

The Library of Congress, Washington, D.C.
Public domain image from the Library of Congress.

TIP #8:

TAKE ADVANTAGE OF TRADE ORGANIZATIONS.

Both for-profit and nonprofit organizations that support independent publishers offer services and opportunities that you should seriously consider looking into. These services include trade shows, award competitions, advertising campaigns, creating and distributing books, PR and marketing, book reviews, business management, education, foreign rights, barcodes, ISBNs, shipping, sales and distribution, and other benefits such as networking with companies and individuals that provide legal services, book design, book printing, audio books, and eBook publishing, to name a few.

The Independent Book Publishers Association (IBPA) is a nonprofit membership organization with nearly 3,000 members, making it the largest publishing trade association in the United States. It hosts the annual Benjamin Franklin Book Awards and the annual Publishing University conference and trade show. IBPA also publishes, for example, an *Industry Standards Checklist for a Professionally Published Book* to give both authors and industry professionals information about the professional presentation recommended for any book.

Independent Publisher hosts the annual Independent Publisher (IPPY) Book Awards. These honor the best independent titles from around the world and recognize thousands of independent, university, and self-published books each year. An "independent" publisher is defined as (a) independently owned and operated; (b) operated by a foundation or university; and (c) long-time independents that eventually incorporated but still operate autonomously and publish fewer than 100 titles a year.

The *Alliance of Independent Authors* (ALLi) is a non-profit membership association for self-publishing authors, providing advice, education, guidance, benefits, and resources, within a friendly and accessible community of successful independent authors and advisors.

The *American Booksellers Association*, is a national nonprofit trade organization that "works with booksellers and industry partners to ensure the success and profitability of independently owned book retailers, and to assist in expanding the community of the book."

Numerous regional independent associations also exist. A partial list is shown below.

• **AuthorYOU®** is a supportive community for you to connect, swap ideas, and learn how to publish, promote, and profit with your books.

• *Bay Area Independent Publishers Association*

• *California Independent Booksellers Alliance*: Promoting the vitality, diversity, and prosperity of independent bookselling.

• *Colorado Independent Publishers Association*

• *Connecticut Authors and Publishers Association*

• *Florida Authors and Publishers Association*

• *Greater New York Independent Publishers Assoc.*

• *Great Lakes Independent Booksellers Association*: Improving the effectiveness of booksellers, forging partnerships among members, promoting the Great Lakes region, and promoting literacy and free speech.

• *Hawaii Book Publishers Association*

• *Independent Publishers of New England*

• *Midwest Independent Booksellers Association*: Supports bookstores and booksellers in Illinois, Iowa, Kansas, Minnesota, Missouri, Nebraska, North Dakota, South Dakota, Wisconsin, and Michigan's UP."

- *Midwest Independent Publishing Association*
- *Minnesota Book Publishers Roundtable*
- *Mountains and Plains Independent Booksellers Assoc*: Professional association of bookstores, booksellers, publishers, authors, and industry professionals, representing hundreds of bookstores across thirteen western and midwestern states.
- *New Atlantic Independent Booksellers Association*: Promoting cooperation and mutual interest among booksellers while advancing their trade.
- *New England Independent Booksellers Association*: Promoting independent bookselling in Connecticut, Maine, Massachusetts, New Hampshire, Rhode Island, Vermont, and New York.
- *Northern California Publishers and Authors*
- *Pacific Northwest Booksellers Association*: Representing the interests of literacy, free speech, and independent bookselling in Alaska, Idaho, Montana, Oregon, and Washington.
- *Publishers and Writers of San Diego*
- *Publishers Association of Los Angeles*
- *Southern Independent Booksellers Alliance*: Represents independent bookstores and booksellers in Florida, South Carolina, North Carolina, Georgia, Louisiana, Alabama, Arkansas, Tennessee, Kentucky, Virginia, and Mississippi.
- *St. Louis Publishers Association*
- *Upper Peninsula Publishers and Authors Assoc.*
- *Writers & Publishers Network:* provides information, resources and opportunities for anyone involved in or interested in publishing.
- **Various** *"Writers Resource Centers"*

A Sampling of Publishing Events

African American Children's Book Fair: one of the oldest and largest single-day events that celebrate Black Americans.

American Library Association Annual Conference: brings together librarians, educators, authors, publishers, etc.

Association of Learned and Professional Society Publishers: (ALPSP) a UK-based trade association.

Association of University Presses Annual Meeting: networking event for university press and nonprofit publishers.

Bologna Children's Book Fair: the leading professional fair for children's books in the world is held in Bologna, Italy.

Book Industry Study Group: trade, education, professional and scholarly publishers, distributors, wholesalers, retailers, manufacturers, service providers and libraries.

Digital Book World: annual gathering of publishing.

ECPA Leadership Summit: where relationships begin and continue among leadership teams in Christian publishing.

Frankfurt Book Fair: important international trade fair for publishing and content of all kinds.

IBPA Publishing University: where hundreds of independent publishers and industry partners gather to exchange knowledge, resources, strategies, solutions, and more.

Kolkata Book Fair: public book fair with over 600 stalls.

London Book Fair: a large trade fair, held in London, England.

Pub West Annual Conference: Pub West is a trade association of small-medium-sized book publishers, printers, editors, distributors, designers, binderies, and related service companies.

Protestant Church-Owned Publishing Association Spring Conference: international association of Protestant denominational publishers and other non-profit Christian publishers.

Society for Scholarly Publishing Annual Meeting: publishers, printers, e-products developers, librarians, editors., and so on.

University Press Week: advances the essential role of a global community of publishers whose mission is to ensure academic excellence and cultivate knowledge.

US Book Show: serves the global bookselling and book publishing industry with top notch programming and online exhibits.

World Book Day: is an annual event organized by the United Nations Educational, Scientific, and Cultural Organization to promote reading, publishing, and copyright.

TIP #9:

BE CAREFUL WHAT YOU WRITE. SOMEONE MIGHT READ IT.

I know that sounds stupid, but it's true. A first-time self-publisher might think that no one is going to read his or her book, so why not insert an off-color joke here and there? That's what I thought when I published my first book, so I sprinkled it with four-letter words appropriate to the subject matter of the book. I did receive a smattering of constructive feedback saying that I used the word "shit" too many times. I don't think you, or any other human being, is ever going to have that problem, but it made me realize not to assume anything when self-publishing.

I even had to defend myself on a witness stand in a court of law where I was an expert witness. The opposing attorney wanted me to explain to the court the chapter title in one of my books. The title was, *"A Day in the Life of a Turd."* It's true that not many people may read your book, but you just don't know who is going to read it, when, and why, and you may be surprised. Assume everyone is going to read it and write it accordingly.

Copyright

You should also be aware of copyright laws, infringement issues, using material from other people, and people using your material, without permission.

According to Copyright.gov, copyright is intellectual property that protects original works of authorship as soon as an author fixes the work in a tangible form of expression. In copyright law, there are a lot of different types of works, including paintings, photographs, illustrations, musical compositions, sound recordings, computer programs, books, poems, blog posts, movies, architectural works, plays, and more.

Everyone is a copyright owner. Once you create an original work and fix it, like taking a photograph, writing a poem or blog, you are the author and the owner. Companies, organizations, and other people besides the work's creator can also be copyright owners. Copyright law allows ownership through "works made for hire," which establishes that works created by an employee within the scope of employment are owned by the employer. The work-made-for-hire doctrine also applies to certain independent contractor relationships for certain types of commissioned works. Copyright ownership can also come from contracts, or from other types of transfers such as wills and bequests.

Furthermore, US copyright law provides copyright owners with the following exclusive rights: (a) to reproduce the work in copies; (b) to prepare derivative works based on the work; (c) to distribute copies of the work to the public by sale or other transfer of ownership or by rental, lease, or lending; (d) to perform the work publicly; and (e) to display the work publicly.

Copyright also provides the owner of the copyright the right to authorize others to exercise these exclusive rights, subject to certain statutory limitations.

The length of copyright protection depends on when a work was created. Under the current law, works created on or after January 1, 1978, have a copyright term of life of the author plus 70 years after the author's death. If the work is a joint work, the term lasts for 70 years after the last surviving author's death. For works made for hire and anonymous or pseudonymous works, copyright protection is 95 years from publication or 120 years from creation, whichever is shorter. Works created before 1978 have a different time frame. The complete list of exemptions to copyright protection can be found in Chapter 1 of Title 17 of the United States Code.

Public Domain

No permission is needed to copy or use public domain works. A work is generally considered to be within the public domain if it is ineligible for copyright protection or its copyright has expired. All works first published or released before January 1, 1927, have lost their copyright protection effective January 1, 2022.

Public domain works may not be protected for a variety of reasons, including the following: (1) the copyright has expired; (2) the work was produced by the US government and is therefore free to use by the general public; (3) the work isn't in a tangible form; (4) the work didn't include a proper copyright notice prior to March 1, 1989. In the US, this doesn't apply to works created after March 1, 1989, when a copyright notice became no longer mandatory to protect a work; (5) the work doesn't have sufficient originality, such as lists or tables from public documents or other common sources.

Fair Use

Fair use is a legal doctrine that promotes freedom of expression by permitting the unlicensed use of copyright-protected works in certain circumstances. Section 107 of the Copyright Act provides the statutory framework for determining whether something is a fair use and identifies certain types of uses — such as criticism, comment, news reporting, teaching, scholarship, and research — as examples of activities that may qualify as fair use. Section 107 calls for consideration of the following four factors in evaluating a question of fair use:

(1) *Purpose and character of the use, including whether the use is of a commercial nature or is for nonprofit educational purposes:* Courts look at how the party claiming fair use is using the copyrighted work, and are more likely to find that nonprofit educational and noncommercial uses are fair. This does not mean, however, that all nonprofit education and noncommercial uses are fair, and all commercial uses are not fair; instead, courts will balance the purpose and character of the use against the other factors below. Additionally, "transformative" uses are more likely to be considered fair. Transformative uses are those that add something new, with a further purpose or different character, and do not substitute for the original use of the work.

(2) *Nature of the copyrighted work:* This factor analyzes the degree to which the work that was used relates to copyright's purpose of encouraging creative expression. Thus, using a more creative or imaginative work (such as a novel, movie, or song) is less likely to support a claim of a fair use than using a factual work (such as a technical article or news item). In addition, use of an unpublished work is less likely to be considered fair.

(3) *Amount and substantiality of the portion used in relation to the copyrighted work as a whole:* Under this factor, courts look at both the quantity and quality of the copyrighted material that was used. If the use includes a large portion of the copyrighted work, fair use is less likely to be found; if the use employs only a small amount, fair use is more likely. That said, some courts have found use of an entire work to be fair under certain circumstances. And in other contexts, using even a small amount of a copyrighted work was determined not to be fair because the selection was an important part — or the "heart"— of the work.

(4) *Effect of the use upon the potential market for or value of the copyrighted work:* Here, courts review whether, and to what extent, the unlicensed use harms the existing or future market for the copyright owner's original work. In assessing this factor, courts consider whether the use is hurting the current market for the original work (for example, by displacing sales of the original) and/or whether the use could cause substantial harm if it were to become widespread.

In addition to the above, other factors may also be considered by a court in weighing a fair use question, depending upon the circumstances. Courts evaluate fair use claims on a case-by-case basis, and the outcome of any given case depends on a fact-specific inquiry. This means that there is no formula to ensure that a predetermined percentage or amount of a work — or specific number of words, lines, pages, or copies — may be used without permission.

Copyright Registration

Copyright exists automatically in an original work of authorship once it is fixed, but a copyright owner can take steps to enhance the protections. The most important step is registering the work. Registering a work is not mandatory, but for US works, registration is necessary to enforce the exclusive rights of copyright through litigation. Timely registration also allows copyright owners to seek certain types of monetary damages and attorney fees if there is a lawsuit, and provide a presumption that information on the registration certificate is correct.

Copyright registration facilitates the licensing marketplace by allowing people to find copyright ownership information, and it provides the public with notice that someone is claiming copyright protection. It also provides a record of this nation's creativity. There is only one place to register claims to copyright in the United States: the Copyright Office. The Copyright Office website, Copyright.gov, is the definitive source of copyright information.

LCCN

What is an LCCN? You will see this on your title page somewhere around the copyright notification and ISBN number. It will look something like "Library of Congress Control Number: 2022012345." These numbers are obtained through the Library of Congress website (LOC.gov). You must first sign up for the Preassigned Control Number Program (PCN program).

Publishers who would like to participate in the PCN Program must first apply for a PCN Publisher Account in the PrePub Book Link (https://www.loc.gov/publish/prepubbooklink/). Once the publisher account has been approved, publishers can begin submitting LCCN requests, and authors can submit an LCCN request after creating an account in PrePub Book Link. Based on the information provided by the author or publisher, library staff assign a preassigned Library of Congress Control Number (LCCN) to each title. The publisher or author prints the LCCN on the title page or copyright page in the following manner: "Library of Congress Control Number: 1234567890."

ISBN

The following is from ISBN-International.org: An ISBN is an International Standard Book Number used by publishers, booksellers, libraries, internet retailers, and other supply chain participants for ordering, listing, sales records, and stock control purposes. The ISBN identifies the registrant as well as the specific title, edition, and format. ISBNs were 10 digits in length up to the end of December 2006, but since January 1st, 2007, they now always consist of 13 digits. It has an associated barcode, which will be located on the back cover of your book.

Each ISBN consists of five elements, with each section being separated by spaces or hyphens:

(1) *Prefix element* — currently this can only be either 978 or 979. It is always 3 digits in length.
(2) *Registration group element* — this identifies the country, geographical region, or language area participating in the ISBN system. This element may be between 1 and 5 digits in length.
(3) *Registrant element* — this identifies the publisher or imprint. This may be up to 7 digits in length.
(4) *Publication element* — identifies the edition and format of a specific title, and may be up to 6 digits.
(5) *Check digit* — this is the final single digit that mathematically validates the rest of the number.

ISBNs are assigned to individual publications rather than to journals, newspapers, or other types of serials. Any book made publicly available, whether for sale or free, can be identified by its ISBN. Each different book form (e.g., paperback, ePub, Kindle Direct Publishing) should have a separate ISBN. The ISBN is an identifier and does not convey any form of legal or copyright protection. However, in some countries the use of an ISBN to identify publications has been made into a legal requirement.

The publisher or self-publisher of the book should apply for the ISBN. The publisher is the group, organization, company, or individual who is responsible for initiating the production of a publication. Normally, it is also the person or body who bears the cost and financial risk in making a product available. It is not normally the printer, but it can be the author of the book if the author has chosen to self-publish.

I get my ISBNs and associated barcodes at Bowker Identifier Services (MyIdentifiers.com). You can also get QR codes there. A "Quick Response Code" (QR code) is a type of barcode that can be scanned using smartphones. You can register and copyright your book at Bowker, publish it through them, and market it through them, if you like. They also provide print book and eBook distribution. Their eBook services distribute through over 40 eBook publishing sites using IngramSpark's platform.

Libel

This information is based on the *Associated Press Style and Libel Guide*. If someone publishes a statement in which a person's reputation is seriously damaged, and that statement is false, and that person is identified in print, even without a name, then libel charges can be brought.

"Libel" is the publication of writing, pictures, cartoons, or any other medium that falsely exposes a person to public hatred, shame, disgrace, or ridicule. Actions for libel are often from news stories that allege crime, fraud, dishonesty, immoral or dishonorable conduct, or stories that defame the subject professionally, causing financial loss either personally or to a business (see the *Associated Press Stylebook and Libel Manual 251*).

To call a person a murderer, a cheat, a child molester, an alcoholic, a liar, a thief, a drug abuser, and so on, can be considered grounds for a libel case. Any accusation that a member of society has violated common standards of ethical behavior can lead to a libel suit. In short, libel is *pub-*

lication of false information about a person that causes injury to that person's reputation.

The difference between libel and slander is: libel refers to any false, defamatory statement *published in writing* while slander is a false statement of defamation *spoken orally*.

The Right to Privacy

From Gallaudet University (Gallaudet.edu): When a person is in a news event, voluntarily or involuntarily, she forfeits some rights to privacy. Similarly, a person involved in a matter of legitimate public interest can be safely written about. However, a story or a picture that dredges up sordid details of a person's past and has no current newsworthiness could be considered libel (see the *Associated Press Stylebook and Libel Manual 261*).

Public figures are generally thought of as people who seek the limelight and inject themselves into public debate. Courts say that involvement in a crime, even a newsworthy one, does not make one a public figure. This is important because if you are proven to be a public figure and someone defames your job performance or ethics, you must prove libel and malicious intent. If you are a private person, you only need to prove libel, but not malicious intent. Consequently, it's easier for private citizens to win a libel case than it is for a public figure to win one.

This is a public domain copyright-free image from Pexels.com, "Woman Leaning On Bookshelf" by Luriko Yamaguchi. All photos and videos on Pexels are free to use; attribution is not required. Crediting the photographer or Pexels is not necessary but always appreciated. You can modify the photos and videos from Pexels. You can be creative and edit them as you like. There are numerous other websites that offer copyright-free images or images for a fee.

TIP #10:

DIVERSIFY.

You can write a book, self-publish it, stop there, and wait for success. It may or may not arrive. On the other hand, you can consider your book a foundation to be built upon. It's a beginning, not an end. This is especially true of non-fiction publications. Nonfiction books often require a lot of research, document review, reading of other related books, travel, interviews of experts in the field, and other work that will likely require years of dedication and effort.

Most research and publishing takes place in the arenas of academia and government. The research is funded by grants and salaries often provided by private corporations through government research agencies. Billionaires contribute big donations to universities and quasi-government agencies, then quietly assert control over how the money is allocated. They are unlikely to support research for anything that is not going to yield them financial benefit.

Some would say that this leaves academia and government 10 years behind the "cutting edge." But it also provides an opportunity for independent researchers to write about subjects that academia and government would rather ignore. Self-publishing can allow a writer to ignore the blockade of censorship deployed by corporations, government, and private interests, and to publish cutting-edge information that would otherwise never see the light of day.

Let's face it, no college professor is going to receive a grant to write a book about turds. However, as an independent publisher, you can glean knowledge and experience that is unique. You can become an expert in a niche field being ignored by everyone else.

A writer can become an expert in even a common field. If you're writing about baby dolls and you've done an impressive amount of research and work on your subject matter, then you are immediately eligible to become a speaker at every baby doll conference, domestic and foreign. You can also spin off other titles related to your topic such as Antique Baby Dolls, or Collectable Baby Dolls. You can figure out where baby doll parts are manufactured, buy them wholesale, and bundle them with your book sales, at retail prices. You can bundle your original Baby Doll Book and your new baby doll books together and sell them discounted in sets, an option that may not be available to your customers through other sellers such as Amazon.

You can become a consultant in baby doll circles. You can testify in court as an expert witness on baby doll matters. You can travel the world finding rare baby dolls for your collection, or just to photograph, measure, and document, all as a business expense and a tax write-off.

I know because I have done, and still do, all of these things. Ironically, I didn't know about these options when I started out. They came to me; I did not seek them.

My first book, a graduate thesis about composting human manure, focused on a topic that no university researcher would touch with a 10-foot shovel. No corporation or billionaire philanthropist would consider funding such research. You can't patent composting.

In 2005, 10 years after the original book came into print, I got a call from a consulting firm in Washington, D.C. They were bidding on an Asian Development Bank project in Mongolia and were confounded about what to do about sanitation in such an impoverished, frigid nation. Would I be willing to go to Mongolia? "Yes, of course," was my immediate answer. I had already been traveling throughout the US and eastern Canada speaking at conferences and advising owners at conference sites and music venues on how to maintain compost sanitation systems, so why not go overseas? I eventually went to Mongolia three times. My experiences there were priceless.

The next request was from Haiti after the earthquake in 2010. I went there four times. Then Africa, where I travelled through six countries over the span of three trips. My compost journeys also included India, Central America, and Europe. I learned a hell of a lot from these experiences and spun off another nonfiction, hardcover book in 2021, *The Compost Toilet Handbook*.

In the midst of all of this, I had also written and self-published a trade industry book, *The Slate Roof Bible*. This is the one I eventually had printed in Hong Kong. The first edition of this book came out in 1997.

In 1998, I got a phone call. Would I go to Washington, D.C., to look at a roof? They were having roof problems and didn't know what to do with the slate roof. They were thinking they needed to tear it off and replace it. I agreed, for a fee, with a written contract with the National Park Service, to go down there to look the roof over.

The building was Ford's Theater, the site where Abraham Lincoln had been assassinated. I accessed the roof through an attic hatch door, needing to walk across planks over the ceiling joists above the stage while a live play was in progress. Pretty interesting job. Turned out the roof was fine. In fact, it had already been replaced. The problems were in segments of the building near the roof, but not part of the roof. I saved the US taxpayer hundreds of thousands of dollars and launched another consulting career that has been ongoing for 24 years, hundreds of roofs, and numerous lawsuits later (I was the expert witness in the lawsuits).

Where do I find time to do all of this, self-publish books, run a business, manage a homestead, raise a family, and travel the world? Short answer: I don't watch TV. I haven't lived in a home with *commercial* television since 1970. As of this writing, that's 52 years. Most people have no idea how much time they waste sitting in front of the brainwashing machine. Just think what you could achieve if you weren't feeding your brain the equivalent of "brain donuts" everyday!

You may realize that most published authors are difficult, if not impossible, to reach directly by phone, email, or postal mail. Everything goes through their publishers first. The publishing firm acts as a firewall of sorts, blocking direct access to the authors and allowing them a degree of privacy in their lives.

If you self-publish, and especially if you diversify, that's not the case. People can reach you in a variety of ways. In some cases, this is good. The phone calls I mentioned above were the tip of the iceberg; a result of my being directly accessible to my readers. On the other hand, I cannot respond to everyone. I always have about 100 emails in my business email inbox. I whittle through them as time allows, but it is impossible to keep up. This is one sacrifice you may be forced to accept as a self-published writer.

Chapter 11

PUBLISHING A PRINT BOOK

How do you get started self-publishing? Let me run you through the process.

1) Write something. Have it edited or proofread by someone other than yourself.

2) Get your manuscript into a page layout software where you can format the text, add images, select the font (letter style), design the interior, and so on. I start out in Word for editing purposes, then cut and paste the content into Quark. I use QuarkXPress, but many use Adobe In-Design. I'm sure there are others.

3) Set up your manuscript.

Page Layout

Most books use a facing-page layout with automatic page numbering placed in a footer.

Margins

Make your inside margin, the one in the center of the book, the gutter, wider than the outside margin. Some designers like a lot of "white space" in their books. I don't, so I set my outside, top, and bottom margins at 1/2″. I set my inside margin at 1 inch on larger books and 3/4″ on smaller ones. This is variable according to your preferences. You can tell what's right by looking at it. The book you're reading now has 1/2″ margins on the top, bottom and outside. The inside margin is 3/4″.

Bleeds

A "bleed" is when your text or color extends off the edge of the page. This is common on covers and in some color images inside the book or magazine. The bleed must be extended approximately 0.125″ past the trim edge of the sheet to ensure a clean-cut edge.

Font

I tend to size my text fonts at 11 points although 12-point text is standard document size; 10 point is a little too small for general reading, in my opinion, although it's fine for quotes and other text that's set apart from the main text. Everyone has his or her own opinion, so by all means choose what works best for you.

Select a font. I've been using Aldine 721 BT, which is what you're looking at now, although there are thousands of different fonts available. You can use separate font styles and sizes for quotes, sidebars, captions, and so on. In this book, I'm using 11-point type for the primary font. In the image captions I'm using Arial 9 point.

When book designers were polled, one of the top choices for the body of a book is the font Caslon, such as Adobe Caslon Pro. Other popular fonts, according to In-gram, are Garamond, Minion, Jenson, and Palatino.

Here's an example of Adobe Caslon Pro.

Here's an example of Adobe Garamond BT.

Here's an example of Adobe Garamond Pro.

Here's an example of Minion Pro.

Here's an example of Palatino Linotype.

Here is Adobe Jensen Pro Regular.

Leading

Adjust the "leading," or the spacing between the lines (pronounced ledding). This was once achieved with strips of lead in the old printing presses, or so I'm told, which is why it's called *leading*. You may find that increasing the leading in your book makes it easier to read. You are now reading 11-point type with 14-point leading. If I had used 11-point leading the lines would be closer together. That means I would have used fewer pages in this book, but the sentences would have seemed a little crowded to my eye. This spacing seems easier to read.

For example, this is 11-point Aldine 721 BT font using 11-point leading. You can see how much closer the lines of type are to each other. Using closer lines will allow you to fit more text on a page, but it also creates a book in which the text is not as easy to read. As the book designer, you have to determine what works best for your book.

Another example: This is 9-point Arial font using 9-point leading. I am using this combination for some image captions. You can see how close the lines are to each other. Again, it is a matter of design preference and personal opinion. You have to determine what works best for your book.

Kerning is the spacing between individual letters or characters. Sometimes you may need to make this adjustment, such as when squeezing words into small spaces.

Trim Size

Choose the size for the book. You'll do this in your page layout software. Printers prefer to use standard sizes because the printing is more efficient and less expensive. My current compost book is 6x9 inches. This book is 5x8 inches; both are standard sizes. For larger books, 8.5x11

MOST COMMON BOOK TRIM SIZES
(from IngramSpark)

General Fiction: 6"x9"

General Nonfiction: 5.5"x8.5"

Thrillers/Mysteries: 5.25"x8"

General Fiction: 5"x7"

Fantasy and Sci-Fi: 5.5"x8.5"

General Self Help: 5.25"x8"

Inspirational/Spiritual: 5"x8"

Memoir: 5.25"x8"

Reference: 6"x9" and 7"x10"

Middle-Grade Fiction: 5"x8"

Children's Picture Books: 8.5"x8.5"

Business: 5.5"x8.25" or 5.25"x8"

BOOK TRIM SIZE OPTIONS
(IngramSpark)

4.000" x 6.000" (152mm x 102 mm)	6.500" x 6.500" (165mm x 165mm)
4.000" x 7.000" (178mm x 102 mm)	6.625" x 10.250" (260mm x 168mm)
4.250" x 7.000" (178mm x 108 mm)	6.690" x 9.610" (244mm x 170mm)
4.370" x 7.000" (178mm x 111mm)	7.000" x 10.000" (254mm x 178mm)
4.720" x 7.480" (190mm x 120mm)	7.440" x 9.690" (246mm x 189mm)
5.000" x 8.000" (203mm x 127mm)	7.500" x 9.250" (235mm x 191mm)
5.000" x 7.000" (178mm x 127mm)	8.000" x 8.000" (203mm x 203mm)
5.060" x 7.810" (198mm x 129mm)	8.000" x 10.000" (254mm x 203mm)
5.250" x 8.000" (203mm x 133mm)	8.000" x 10.880" (276mm x 203mm)
5.500" x 8.500" (216mm x 140mm)	8.250" x 11.000" (280mm x 210mm)
5.500" x 8.380" (213mm x 140mm)	8.250" x 10.750" (273mm x 210 mm)
5.500" x 7.500" (191mm x 140mm)	8.268" x 11.693" (297mm x 210mm) A4
5.500" x 8.250" (210mm x 140mm)	8.500" x 11.000" (280mm x 216mm)
5.830" x 8.270" (210mm x 148mm) A5	8.500" x 8.500" (216mm x 216mm)
6.000" x 9.000" (229mm x 152mm)	8.500" x 9.000" (229mm x 216mm)
6.140" x 9.210" (234mm x 156mm)	11.000" x 8.500" (216mm x 280mm)

inches is a standard size. Standard sizes waste less paper.

My first book, the execrable one, had a trim size of 9"h x 7.25"w. You will notice from the chart on the opposite page that this is not standard. Although the next edition had a new cover design, a four-page color insert, and expanded from 198 pages to 302 pages, the trim size was 9"h x 7"w, still not standard. Both editions sold for $19.

The bottom line is that it was too expensive to print. What I've learned is that the cover price of a book should be about ten times more than the print cost. A $20 book should cost a maximum of $2 to print. By the time all the "middle men" take their cut, the distributor, bookstores, and so on, you are netting a third of the cover price. A $20 book will net *maybe* $6.50. Subtract your reprinting cost from that, and you have $4.50 to cover remaining expenses.

In my case, my $19 book was costing about $3 to print, which is financially unwise. I would net about $6 from each book sale, less the $3 reprinting cost, yielding $3 per book to cover the costs of doing business. It's difficult to stay in business with such slim profit margins, so I was considering letting the book go out of print.

Instead, I decided to try a new strategy. I would publish a third edition, change it to a standard trim size (6"x9"), take out the color pages, and edit out everything repetitive, redundant, and unnecessary. I ended up with a 255-page book, then I raised the price from $19 to $25.

What happened? I sold 41,000 copies of the third edition over a 10-year time span. This alone adds up to over a million dollars in cover price sales. Each book netted about $8. By changing the book specifications, I dropped the average printing cost per book down to about $1.26. The strategy worked, and now I was back in business.

LCCN, ISBN

Once the manuscript is finished and you have a book size, binding style (hardcover or softcover), page count, and retail price, you can assign your International Standard Book Number. These factors must be determined before applying for the ISBN. You can order the ISBN online through Bowker (MyIdentifiers.com).

You can order the Library of Congress Control Number online, too (https://www.loc.gov/publish/pcn/). For this book, it took exactly four days for me to apply for an LCCN online and to receive it via email. Plug these numbers into your title page and provide the ISBN's associated barcode to your cover artist for placement on the book cover. The EAN-13 bar code must be located on the bottom right corner (next to the spine) of the back cover.

The ISBN, or European Article Number (EAN), is a 12- or 13-digit product identification code that identifies the product, manufacturer, and price. A UPC (Universal Product Code) was the original format for barcodes in the 1970s. Eventually, growing international use of barcodes required 13 digits to allow for country of origin coding.

Many self-publishing platforms offer authors the opportunity to use a free ISBN. However, if you don't purchase the ISBN yourself, your own publishing company will not be associated with your book. If you use a free ISBN through a service, it will hold the service's "imprint," or publisher identity, not yours. Not purchasing an ISBN yourself may also limit where you can print and distribute your own title. For example, a book with a Kindle eBook ISBN, is probably not going to be published anywhere but on Kindle. It's in your best interest to be recognized as the owner of your work, which is why we publishers should purchase our own ISBNs.

Printer

Now you need a printer. If it's a book, you will need a book printer, an eBook publisher, and/or an audiobook service. You can solicit for quotes from several printers at once and compare them. They will need to know paper type, if the interior is color or black and white, trim size, page count, cover type, how many copies, and so on.

Some printers cater to self-publishers and will happily do small print runs. Although I have used a number of printers over the years, one company that I find easy to work with is McNaughton & Gunn, a Michigan-based printer that has been producing book titles since 1975. I'll use them as an example here, although a simple computer search will lead you to a lot of acceptable printers. Trade associations also list printers among their members.

M&G states: "We understand that printing your book is an investment and that its physical appearance can influence its success. As a result, you need access to self-publisher resources that can help guide you along your journey. We provide first-time publisher resources that can assist you with everything from design, eBook conversion, to prepping your files for upload. We can promote your book."

I have also had good results from Kindle Direct Publishing, where you can print small runs of print-on-demand books and receive an author price when ordering up to 999 books at a time. IngramSpark is yet another option.

Offset Book Printing

This works best for customers who:
    (a) Need larger print runs (lowering the unit cost)
    (b) Require an exact color for cover or insert
    (c) Prefer a traditional printing technique
    (d) Prefer additional paper and cover options

M&G offset book printing specifications include:
  (a) Print runs from 250 to 50,000+
  (b) Schedules based on specifications and needs
  (c) 4x6 inches minimum; 9x12 inches maximum
  (d) One- and two-color ink for text
  (e) Choices in soft or hard covers
  (f) Four-color (CMYK) covers and inserts
  (g) A variety of white and natural papers
  (h) Page counts divisible by 8
  (i) Print-ready PDF files are preferred

Short Run Digital Printing

This works best for customers who:
  (a) Need smaller quantities or advanced reader copies
  (b) Need to fill the gap until new editions are printed
  (c) Need to fill quick orders
  (d) Need to better manage inventory

M&G short run digital specification options include:
  (a) Print runs from 25 to 750
  (b) 4″ x 6″ minimum; 8½″ x 11″ maximum
  (c) Black ink or color for text
  (d) Four-color covers
  (e) Perfect (soft) binding.
  (f) Gloss or matte film lamination on cover
  (g) Many paper options
  (h) Page counts divisible by 2
  (i) 10-or 12-point coated-1-side (C1S) cover stock

Paper Types

Paper types for books range roughly from 50 pound to 100 pound, which indicates the thickness as well as the weight. You will need to know your page count and what paper you're going to use in order to calculate the thickness of the spine of the book. This measurement is necessary when designing the cover art.

Paper finishes include smooth, antique, eggshell, opaque, and lynx white. The printer can send you samples of the paper types and weights.

Four-Color (CMYK) pages can print on 60# white, 70# white, 70# matte, and 80# gloss. Some printers will print "premium" color books on 70# 378 PPI white paper, and "standard" color books on 50# 512 PPI white paper. PPI stands for "pages per inch."

There are two common ways paper stock is measured: *pounds* and *points*, usually seen as "#" or "lb" when referring to pounds, and a simple "pt" for points. Pounds refers to the weight of the paper. The thicker the paper is, the higher the weight is likely to be. These weights typically range between 20 and 140 pounds per ream of paper. Usually, 500 sheets of paper make up a ream.

Points measure the thickness of the paper rather than the weight. The higher the points value, the thicker the paper. A 10-point paper is 10/1000ths of an inch in thickness, while 16-point paper is 16/1000ths of an inch.

Coated stocks include gloss coated and silk (matte) coated. The most common weights for gloss and matte cover stocks are from 80 to 130 pounds, and from 80 to 100 pounds for texts. Full-color books are usually printed on coated paper for better quality images.

Uncoated stock weights range from 65 to 130 pounds for covers, and 40 to 100 pounds for texts.

Common Text Paper Weights

50 lb: novels, workbooks, paperbacks, and most documents; roughly equivalent to standard copy paper

70 lb: comic books, large catalogs

80 lb: magazines, catalogs, booklets, hardcover books

100 lb: children's, art, comic book covers, brochures

Typical Paper Types

40# Alternative Book Vellum, 500 PPI

40# Alternative Book Cream, 400 PPI

45# Alternative Book Cream, 400 PPI   454 PPI

50# Enviro Book White Recycled, 100% PCW, FSC Certified,

55# Enviro Book Natural Recycled, 100% PCW, FSC Certified,

50# Natural Antique, FSC Certified, 400 PPI   416 PPI

50# Natural Offset Eggshell, FSC Certified, 500 PPI

55# Natural Offset Antique, FSC Certified, 360 PPI

60# Natural Offset Eggshell, FSC Certified, 420 PPI

50# White Offset Smooth, FSC Certified, 512 PPI

60# White Offset Smooth, FSC Certified, 435 PPI

70# White Offset Smooth, FSC Certified, 370 PPI

50# White Offset Vellum, FSC Certified, 476 PPI

60# White Offset Vellum, FSC Certified, 400 PPI

70# Matte White, FSC Certified, 526 PPI

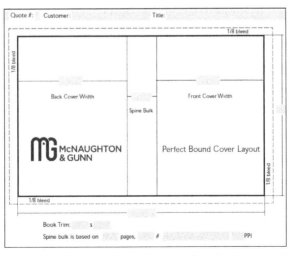

Printers will provide cover templates.

Common Cover Paper Weights

10-point (100 lb): One of the lightest cover stocks available, good for catalog covers or smaller perfect-bound projects such as handbooks. Ten-point covers are too thin for many trade paperback books and can curl easily.

12-point (110 lb): This is a more common cover stock for paperbacks, graphic novels, and other larger perfect-bound covers. This is usually C1S (coated on one side with either a glossy or matte film). The book you're now reading has a 12-point cover coated one side with a glossy film.

16-point (130 lb): This is a heavy cover for catalogs, trade paperbacks, and oversize perfect-bound products.

Here are specs from two of my book printings:

Title: *Humanure Handbook,* 4th Ed (2021)
Binding: Perfect bound, hinge score (spine = 0.65″)
Trim Size: 6.0000″ x 9.0000″; Total Pages: 304
Printing: Black (no text bleeds, no tight margins)
Paper: 50# Enviro Book, 454 PPI (FSC)
Cover: 12PT C1S (FSC), 4-Color Process (4/0), Gloss Film
Files: High-Quality PDF files
Packing: Packing Cartons, maximum 35 pounds

Title: *Compost Toilet Handbook* (2022)
Binding: P.U.R. Adhesive Case Bound, Lithocase over 0.098 Binder Board (hardcover)
Trim Size: 6.0000″ x 9.0000″, **Pages:** 256; **Printing:** Four color; **Paper:** 80# Gloss 556 PPI

Note that the 80# gloss paper is thinner (556 pages/inch) than the 50# Enviro Book (454 pages/inch), although gloss paper is heavier due to the gloss coating. The coating allows for higher quality color printing.

Bindings

PUR binding: A method of adhesive book binding known for its strong, durable finish. The adhesive used for PUR binding is polyurethane reactive (hence PUR). A layer of adhesive is spread across the spine, with a cover mounted over the top to bind the sections to the cover.

Perfect Binding (softcovers): Typically employ ethylene vinyl acetate (EVA) adhesives, which are considered weaker than polyurethane reactive (PUR).

Litho-Wrap Case Binding (hardcover): Allows your protected print cover to be bound directly to the hard cover, attaching it to your book forever, for a lower price than standard case binding with a dust jacket. Litho-wrapped covers can have a gloss or matte laminate, although matte can scuff easily. While this was once a popular binding for textbooks, it has become popular with children's books and novels.

A Final Word about Print Books

Brace yourself for the harsh reality about publishing print books. If you're a self-publisher and you want to suceed as a business, your book content must have a willing audience. *You must provide information that people want to read.* Popular authors published by the big firms have a team of promotors and advertisers pushing their work. You probably don't. If you have important information, a compelling story, a timely account, an endearing tale, or a fun read, you're good to go. Proceed with caution and understand your competition. Creating a book is like folding up a paper airplane. When you throw it out there, will it fly? Start small, don't break your bank, and you'll soon be chasing your dream, like a paper airplane adrift in the wind.

Chapter 12

PUBLISHING AN EBOOK

You can increase your book's readership by offering it as both a print book and an eBook. Kindle is a type of eBook, but this format can only be read on Kindle devices. If your book is only on Kindle, then people who use other eBook devices can't read it.

If readers only buy print books at their local bookstore, they won't have access to your eBook either. Many eBook readers, on the other hand, regularly purchase print books. They'll have physical print books at home, to read in the evening, in their favorite chair, but they may want eBooks while traveling with their laptops, tablets, and smartphones, most of which are far lighter than physical print books. eBook devices are portable and convenient and can sometimes fit in your pocket. It's important that you create your book in as many formats as possible and make it available to as many readers as you can.

Converting a Print Book to eBook

IngramSpark (for example) offers a convenient eBook conversion service for print titles in your IngramSpark account. It is not expensive to convert your existing print book into an eBook. When you use IngramSpark's ePub conversion service, they format your eBook for you, guaranteeing its compatibility with all eBook channels.

eBook Formats

ePub is the most common format for eBooks. If you use a Sony Reader, a Nook, Kindle, Kobo, or an iPad, you can download the ePub file format. The format is reflowable, so it is easily read on a variety of applications and devices. ePub allows a wide range of possibilities regarding multimedia options in your eBook. You can include additional tools and resources in your eBook that would not be available in your print copy. ePub has several newer versions that have more multimedia capabilities to explore (ePub 2 and ePub 3). If you're going to spend time and energy converting your book to only one reflowable eBook format, ePub is the most versatile and will be most easily read on all the major devices.

MOBI can be read by the Kindle, Kobo, and Kindle DX. This is a fixed format eBook originally designed for reading files on mobile phones with lower bandwidth.

PDF files can be read by almost all desktop computers, as well as tablets and smartphones. You will need to install Adobe Acrobat Reader or another PDF reading application to view the PDF. A book converted into PDF format will look exactly like the original print book. PDF books can be readily downloaded from websites, either free or for a fee. This is a good way to make your entire book, unaltered, available to the public as an electronic version.

I have used PDF eBooks almost exclusively because my books tend to be heavily illustrated and are not easily "reflowable." However, books that contain mostly text are easily converted into all eBook formats.

iBook files can be read by the iPad and iPad mini devices. If you use these devices, you can download the iBook file format.

Kindle has its own preferred eBook format, which uses both reflowable and fixed formatting. The Kindle Package Format (KPF) is the format Kindle says best fits across their eReader devices. This format has a wide range of capabilities, available as a reflowable format or as a fixed format. To format your book into a KPF file, download the free app *Kindle Create*. While a KPF file is great for Kindle, it isn't widely accepted elsewhere. You will need to format your book again in different formats for it to be available through other retailers.

TXT (Plain Text): Platforms include Kobo, Kindle supported, and Nook. The format is reflowable. TXT is a file that only supports text. While it isn't a fancy eBook format, if you want to format your book of words without pictures to be read on an eReader, TXT will do the job for most eReader devices.

Fixed Format and a Reflowable Format

Fixed Format: An easy example of a fixed format is a PDF, where the document looks the same, with the same word and picture placing, regardless of what device you're reading it on. It will always appear on a screen just as it would appear in the print book. Fixed format books are great for books that rely heavily on images.

Reflowable Format: This format creates a document that is able to flow, change, and shift appearance to best fit how it is being viewed, such as from a phone, a tablet, or a computer screen. The reader may change the size of the text, the font, or the color to read it more easily. Books with a lot of text are good in a reflowable format because changing the text size or font doesn't change the book.

Converting your Book

Online book retailers will provide specific resources and tips for book formatting, including instructional PDF downloads as well as instructional videos. Let's take a look at two of the more popular eBook publishers, IngramSpark, and Kindle.

IngramSpark

Your electronic book content must first be uploaded into a portal so that it can be processed and then distributed to online retailers. There are a few rules that must be followed to ensure the successful processing of your book's content with IngramSpark.

For every eBook title, two files should be uploaded: one complete interior ePub file (formatted as .epub), and one complete front cover (formatted as .jpeg or .jpg). Interior files must be 100MB or less, formatted as ePub 2 or 3 (flowable text). IngramSpark accepts fixed layouts, but these books will only be available to Apple and Kobo. No single image inside an ePub can be greater than 4 million pixels. Total pixels = length in pixels x width in pixels.

Include an internal cover image. This should be formatted the same size as your interior, for use within the book's content.

Be sure the metadata entered in IngramSpark matches the information on the cover.

There should not be any reference to page numbers in the book. This includes the table of contents! Your flowable eBook will never look just like your print book. eReaders are limited in the way they display content, and your book will appear different from device to device.

Book cover files for display on retail partners' websites

must contain the front cover only. Full-spread print book jackets that include spine and back cover will be rejected. The format must be a JPG file, a maximum of 2,560 pixels on longest side, and a minimum of 1,600 pixels on shortest side. All front covers must be RGB. The content of the cover image must not infringe on another publisher's or artist's copyright.

You can create your eBook's cover and interior using IngramSpark's free book-building tool.

All versions of a title that will be distributed must be supplied with a unique ISBN-13 number. The eBook edition would have a unique ISBN-13, different from the print edition.

When an updated or revised file is uploaded for a title already submitted to IngramSpark, the new version replaces the older version. The new file goes through the same "ingestion" process as the original file and will become the version distributed to the retail partners for purchase or download. IngramSpark eBook ingestion is fully automated, with little or no human intervention as the files are processed through their system.

For self-publishers, formatting a book's content can be frustrating. If you're not experienced in creating digital content or don't have access to book layout software, consider enlisting the help of a professional book designer or use IngramSpark's free book-building tool.

It's also recommended that a professional copyeditor review your manuscript before the design phase begins. You will want all changes to be made to your manuscript before you format or upload your eBook files.

You can calculate *library pricing* in your IngramSpark account when setting up a new eBook or updating pricing on existing eBooks. This makes it possible for your eBooks to be distributed to IngramSpark's library partners. Library pricing for eBooks is typically 2.5 times the eBook's retail price. If you're selling your eBook for $10.00 to eBook retailers, you can charge $25.00 as your library price.

Kindle eBook Manuscript Formatting Guide

The info below is specific to Microsoft Word 2016, but the steps are similar to other versions of Word. For directions on how to format your eBook manuscript using Mac, search online for "Publishing for Mac Users." *Amazon Kindle Direct Publishing* provides users of Apple computers a number of convenient methods for publishing eBooks in Kindle format. Or just go to kdp.amazon.com.

Use *Kindle Create* (PC or Mac) to transform your completed manuscript into a Kindle eBook. This tool creates an active table of contents by automatically detecting and styling chapter titles. It works with several word processing applications that can export to .doc(x) format, such as Microsoft Word, Apple Pages, and Google Docs.

Use *Cover Creator* to create an attractive cover with a stock photo from Kindle's image gallery; or upload an image from your computer. You'll be able to choose a layout, color scheme, and font that best reflects your book's content. The Cover Creator tool also allows you to preview your cover before you publish.

There's a big difference between a finished manuscript and a formatted file that's ready to upload to KDP. For the best results, use these recommended tools.

Additional Design Considerations

Paragraph spacing: In most cases, there should not be a line of space between paragraphs. Indicate the beginning of a new paragraph by indenting the first line. The first line paragraph indent in this book is 1/4".

Space above a paragraph can be used sparingly to indicate a new section. Whenever there is a blank line above a paragraph, you can eliminate the first-line indent on that paragraph, if you so desire.

Widows and orphans: The first line of a paragraph shouldn't fall on the last line of a page, and the last line of a paragraph should not go over to the top of the next page. Widowed and orphaned lines interrupt the flow of reading, thereby impeding reading comprehension. Just remember it this way: a *widow* is something left alone at the end of something. An *orphan* is something left alone at the beginning of something.

Subheadings: These are section titles that have text smaller in size than the chapter title but larger or bolder than the text on your pages. They stand out, they attract attention, and they make it easier for the reader to find subject matter. When a subheading appears at the bottom of a page, it should be followed by at least two lines of text.

Word stacks: When the same word appears in the same position in three or more consecutive lines, this is called a "word stack." These are removed by adjusting word spacing or editing the text.

A **Widow** seems abandoned and alone at the end of something. These look unprofessional, leaving too much white space at the end of a section. An **Orphan** is abandoned and alone at the beginning of something. They look unprofessional, they break the flow of reading, and they belong on the previous page.

ORPHAN

phrases.
Words, sentences, phrases, questions, statements, poetry, comments, words, sentences, phrases, questions, statements, poetry, comments, words, sentences, phrases, questions, statements, poetry, comments, words, sentences, phrases, questions, statements, poetry, comments, words, sentences, phrases, questions, statements, poetry, comments, words, sentences, phrases, questions, statements, poetry, comments, words, sentences, phrases, questions, statements, poetry, comments, words, sentences, phrases, questions, statements, poetry, comments, words, sentences, phrases, questions, statements, poetry, comments, words, sentences, phrases, questions, statements, poetry, comments, words, sentences, phrases, questions, statements, poetry, comments, words, sentences, phrases, questions, statements, poetry, comments, words, sentences, **phrases**.

WIDOW

A **widow** is a short line – possibly one word, at the end of a paragraph or column. A widow leaves too much white space between paragraphs or at the bottom of a page. It is also a paragraph-ending line that falls at the beginning of the following page, separated from the rest of the text.

An **orphan** is a single word, part of a word, or very short line, appearing at the beginning of a column or a page. It is also the first line of a paragraph stranded at the bottom of a page.

Chapter 13

Now What?

Who's going to read it? Why would anyone want to read *your* book? That's an exact quote from a relative in response to my telling them that I was going to publish a book. And no, it wasn't my cousin Larry. It was my (former) mother-in-law.

Chances are, you'll hear the same sort of commentary. You're not a celebrity. You're not a presidential candidate, or a famous actor or actress. You're not a famous writer. Why would anyone read something you, a nobody, wrote? Who would do that?

Well, I'll tell you again who's going to read it. If you don't publish it — *no one*. Nobody. That's who. *If* you don't publish your work, nobody will even know it exists. So how could they read it, even if they would want to?

If a book is worth taking the time and effort to write, then it's worth reading, at least to some people. Letting those people know that the book exists is a large part of self-publishing.

A book isn't *published* until it's made available to readers. How successful it is depends a lot on you, the author. This is when you pull on that thick skin, practice shameless self-promotion, and start getting your book out into the public eye.

Where do you start? Well, when you hire a printer, they may have distribution options. If you're "printing on demand," you won't have to warehouse boxes of books. If you're printing larger book runs, the books have to be stored somewhere. Some printers also offer fulfillment services (they will ship your books), design services, eBook conversion, book promotion, distribution, and marketing.

Ten Marketing Suggestions

(1) Ask friends to leave reviews on Amazon and elsewhere. Send them a book, email them the links to the books, and hope for the best.

(2) Locate other authors, and ask them to review and endorse your book.

(3) Start posting about your book on social media sites, your own and others.

(4) Start a blog or write a guest post for other blogs.

(5) Offer to speak or be interviewed on podcasts.

(6) Develop an Amazon Author page.

(7) Accumulate a mailing list, and send videos and other information about your product(s).

(8) Search for relevant conferences and organizations that may provide opportunities for presentations and public speaking.

(9) Look for opportunities to reach radio and TV studios. They're always looking for fresh material to fill their broadcast days.

(10) Send press releases to your local newspapers. They may print your press release, or they may want to interview you in person. Do the releases professionally. Limit your press release to one page. Include a photo or two and a license so the papers can use them if they want to.

Independent publishing organizations offer advertising opportunities, often targeting libraries, bookstores, and other reliable book buyers, both domestic and international. They also offer book competitions.

For example, IngramSpark suggests a 21-day book marketing plan that can be downloaded from their website.

And don't forget the three main rules about promotion: follow up, follow up, follow up. If you're not getting any results, make phone calls. Maybe the newspapers or radio stations never received your promotional material. Maybe your promo got lost in the shuffle. Maybe the people who can help you are just too busy and your promo material got stuck in a stack in the corner of the desk. Call them. Send it again if you must. Meet them in person if you can.

Book Competitions

If your book can win an award, it becomes an "award-winning book." In order for your book to win awards, you have to enter it into book competitions. As a self-publisher, you have a unique opportunity here because you may only have one book at a time to work with. This makes it easy to enter the book into competitions, as opposed to a larger publisher who may have dozens of books being published at the same time. Why is this an issue? Because it costs money to enter books into book competitions.

For example, the Benjamin Franklin Book Awards, hosted by the Independent Book Publishers Association (IBPA), costs $95 per entry in 2022 for members (for non-members it's $229 for the initial entry; $95 for additional entries). If you have one book and you want to enter it into three categories to increase your chances of winning, it will cost a member 3 x $95.

Some books won't fall into one particular category and

have an increased chance of winning if they're entered in more than one category. A book about poop doesn't fit neatly into any available category. It could be in the "gardening" category, but it won't win against the beautiful coffee table gardening books that it has to compete against. It could win in the "environmental" category, if there is one, or maybe the "science" category. Gotta play to win.

The IPPY Awards, sponsored by *Independent Publisher*, is open to independent authors and publishers worldwide who produce books intended for an English-speaking audience. "Independent" is defined as (a) independently owned and operated (no title limit); (b) operated by a foundation or university (no title limit); or (c) long-time independents that became conglomerated but operate autonomously and publish fewer than 100 titles a year.

In 2022, the IPPY awards had 90 subject categories; received about 5,000 entries from the US, Canada, Australia, New Zealand, the Pacific Rim, and Europe; and issued approximately 400 awards. To win one of those awards out of such a large pool of competition is truly an honor, especially when you consider that the entries are the cream of the crop in independent publishing.

Winners and finalists who compete in higher-quality award competitions can attend an award ceremony and

A Sampling of Independent Book Competitions in the US:

Benjamin Franklin Book Awards
Beverly Hills Book Awards
Eric Hoffer Book Awards
Foreword Magazine Book of the Year Awards
Great Midwest Book Festival
Independent Press Awards
Independent Publisher Book Awards
National Indie Excellence Awards
New England Book Festival
New York Book Festival
Readers' Favorite Awards
Top Shelf Book Awards
Writer's Digest Self-Published Book Awards
Writers Notes Book Awards

celebration party where they can receive gold, silver, or bronze medals; award stickers for their book covers; award certificates; and national publicity through press releases, as well as social media exposure. These are great places to meet people, too, or just to have a good time with like-minded people. Have your photo taken at the award ceremony, and send it out in press releases.

Distribution

What is a book distributor, and how does that work? Let's say you've published a book and a bookstore wants to buy 50 copies. They're entitled to a discount off the cover price of 40 to 60 percent. They're going to buy your $10 book for $4.50. Are they offered free shipping as well, or do they pay for the shipping costs? What about returns? If the books sit on their shelves for six months and they still have 25 copies remaining, can they return them and get their money back?

Do you want to distribute the book yourself, or do you want to hire a book distributor to handle this part of the business? If you're a self-published author, maybe you want to spend your time writing additional books and leave the distribution to someone else. If a professional book distributor handles your sales and shipments, they will take an additional percentage of the gross sales.

If you're printing books in quantities, maybe thousands, then they will need to be warehoused somewhere. Will you be taking responsibility for that, or will your book distributor do it? If the distributor handles warehousing, there may be an additional charge per book for storage.

A professional distributor has all of the connections in the book trade that you do not have. They sell to Amazon; Barnes & Noble; and all of the bookstores, libraries, and universities, as well as to individuals.

You will have a distribution agreement with your distributor, a contract that lays out the stipulations of your professional relationship. For example, in my distribution agreement, I must allow all sales to the book trade to take place through my distributor. However, I am able to provide direct sales to customers who are not bookstores. I sell books directly on my website, both retail and wholesale, but the vast majority of my book sales occur through my distributor, and the number-one buyer is Amazon.

I know what you're wondering: *How do I get a book distributor?* You will need to do some research and determine what publishers produce books of a similar genre. Do they also provide distribution services for self-publishers? If so, determine the person who would be your contact there and send him or her a copy of your book with a cover letter.

That book can be a finished first printing, or you can do a limited pre-publication review edition for the purpose of soliciting for reviews, for promotional opportunities, and to obtain distribution. If your book shows promise, someone will want to review it, someone will want to interview you about it, and someone will want to distribute it. Follow up on any solicitations.

Alternatively, you can self-publish through such outfits as Kindle or IngramSpark. Here they will print and distribute books for you. The books will likely be "print on demand" editions where storage and warehousing are not needed, saving you money.

My architectural book was printed in Hong Kong twice. The second printing was delivered to me by tractor trailer in a shipping container holding ten pallets. The books weighed 20,000 pounds (10 tons). The retail value of the second printing alone was $245,000. Luckily, I have a secure warehouse where I can store them. When my book distributor runs low on stock, they let me know, and I ship them more books, usually by LTL tractor trailer load on a pallet (LTL means "less than a truck load").

When I drafted my first book, a modified graduate thesis, as I have mentioned numerous times already, I really did think that nobody would be interested in it other than the occasional oddball who would force me to go out to my garage and dig a copy out of a moldy box. I couldn't even get a close friend, a professional artist, to draw illustrations for the book; he thought it was that bad. Despite the discouraging influences, I self-published the book anyway. After all, who's going to read it if it isn't published? You already know the answer to that. Nobody.

That single book, printed in the USA, has already sold enough copies to total over 1.6 million dollars in retail sales. If I had chickened out and not published it, I would not be able to make that statement today. And this is not a boast about money — not at all. The benefits of books go far beyond the dollar value of book sales.

My thesis book took me on adventures to Mongolia (three times), Haiti (four times), Mozambique, Morocco, Finland (four times), Kenya, Tanzania, Uganda, India, Nicaragua, eastern Canada, and all over the US. All of these trips were on business matters related to the book's content. Some were speaking engagements, some were consulting trips, some were research trips, some were paid for on a contract agreement; the rest I paid for myself, as business expenses from the money the book generated.

Since my first book was about poop, in particular about compost toilets, and since billions of people don't have toilets (believe it or not), I was able to teach people in underdeveloped countries how to make odorless, environmental toilets that they could place beside their beds or in any other comfortable indoor space. No need to go outside to a hole in the ground anymore, as they had done for centuries.

The most common reaction I received from these people was, "*I didn't know you could do this. I have never heard about this. I didn't know it was possible.*" This simple improvement in their daily existence was life changing. It brought tears to the eyes of some. Yes, we self-publishers, the lepers of the literary world according to some mainstream publications, can write and publish information that will dramatically change people's lives for the better. In some cases, we may even change the world.

The ability to make revolutionary changes in the lives of impoverished people around the world was a by-product of my own self-publishing. There is no monetary value that can be placed on something of this nature. The experiences have been priceless.

What awesome experiences are waiting for you?

NOTES

About the Author

Joseph Jenkins self-published his first book in 1995 as a modified graduate thesis. The nonfiction *Humanure Handbook* went through four editions (the 4th in 2019), was presented with numerous book awards, and is still an active title in the book trade. It has been translated and published in six foreign language print books with additional translations pending, plus an additional 12 foreign languages as full or partial eBook downloads.

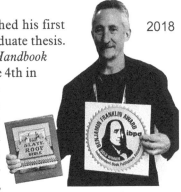

2018

His second self-published book, the nonfiction *Slate Roof Bible*, now in its third edition (full-color hardcover), published in 2016, has received numerous book awards.

Jenkins self-published *The Balance Point*, in two editions, in the "creative nonfiction" genre. The second edition (2018) was presented with several book awards.

He also self-published the nonfiction *Slate Roofs 1926* in 2020, a modified reproduction of a public domain book originally published in 1926, as well as the nonfiction *Compost Toilet Handbook* in 2021, a full-color hardcover book.

Jenkins, who has traveled to over 60 countries, is executive director of the non-profit trade association the Slate Roofing Contractors Association of North America Inc., and has operated a for-profit business in the building trades continually since 1970, incorporating in 2003 as Joseph Jenkins Inc. He is also an organic gardener and grandfather.

JosephJenkins.com

Index